ACTIONABLE
LIFE SKILLS
for
TEENS &
YOUNG ADULTS

A PRACTICAL ROADMAP TO SUCCESS

MAYA
SHINE

ISBN: 978-1-7382033-5-2 (paperback)   ISBN: 978-1-7382033-9-0 (ebook)
ISBN: 978-1-7382033-7-6 (hardcover)   ISBN: 978-1-7382033-4-5 (audio book)

Contributors: Thomas Hauck, Hazel Shahgholi, Jeremy Cloud, Red Cloud
Cover design: Massinissa Aberkane
Text layout: Peggy Stockdale

Questions or comments? Contact the publisher at:
flona.publishing@gmail.com

Dedication

Praise be to God, who blessed me with unexpected gifts, led me through unforeseen paths, and helped me see the light where I could not perceive it.

Maya, your sparkling spirit has been my wonderful source of inspiration. This book is your legacy, a reminder always to shine, no matter the challenges you will face.

My heartfelt thanks to the talented team who helped me take this project to new heights. Alone, we might move faster, but together, we've gone even further!

With sincere gratitude,

Maya Shine

Contents

Preface

When I was a young adult, I had many questions and very few places to look for answers. So I decided to write this book, because it's the one I would have wanted and needed.

First, a little bit about me. With a background in computer engineering, a master's degree in administration, and a couple of certifications in information security, I have spent the past two decades in various roles as a consultant, team leader, and manager. However, my most important role is that of a mother to a daughter on the brink of adolescence—the critical stage of life that you, too, find yourself within.

When I left the safety of my home at 18 to pursue my college education, I was unprepared for the vastness of the world outside. Overwhelmed and often in tears, I quickly realized the lack of fundamental skills necessary to thrive independently. Despite her best efforts, my mother, a strong single parent raising five children, could not provide me with the guidance and preparation I needed to face the real world.

For years, I struggled to find my footing, learning important life lessons through trial and error. It was a challenging journey, but eventually, I found my way. Now, as a mother myself, and a world citizen, I feel the responsibility to equip my daughter—and young adults like you—with the knowledge and skills required for a successful transition into independence and thriving adulthood.

I write this book with special thoughts for young adults who face difficult circumstances, such as being raised by a single parent, growing up without parental figures, facing incarceration, or being neurodivergent. I sincerely wish to inspire hope within you; we can all succeed and thrive despite tribulations in our circumstances.

Why is it important to me to help you achieve your goals? Because we are all part of a global village, and it takes the collective effort of the community to raise exceptional individuals like you! By planting seeds of knowledge, empowerment, and self-sufficiency in the global community, we can shape a brighter future for all. Each positive change we inspire has a ripple effect, impacting lives far beyond our understanding.

What's in it for you? Save yourself the time and hassle of figuring out everything on your own; spare yourself the hardships of trial and error. Together, we will lay the foundations for your well-being, financial independence, and self-sufficiency, enabling you to take control of your future and thrive.

May this book empower you, guide you, and ultimately help you achieve fulfillment.

Sincerely,

Maya Shine

Introduction

*D*id you know that according to a recent survey, 81 percent of new college graduates wish they had been taught more life skills before they got their diploma? In particular, they have little knowledge of how to invest, make long-term financial plans, and manage their student loan debt.

How about everyday money management? Many educated young people regret not being taught how to make a simple household budget.[1]

Life skills are different from academic knowledge. You can ace every class in high school and college and still not know how to make your own dinner or pay your phone bill. Life skills are just that—the skills you need to be independent and self-sufficient.

Life skills improve your job prospects, too. Employers look for people who have not only relevant experience, but all-round life or "soft skills". A research study revealed that nearly 75 percent of employers say they have difficulty finding graduates with the life skills their companies need.[2]

Do you feel like you need to learn more life skills so that you can lead an independent life? Are you still living at home and want to support yourself? Or perhaps you're already on your own and just feel a little overwhelmed. If so, you've come to the right place!

The purpose of this book is very simple: to provide you with straightforward, no-nonsense information about the life skills and knowledge you'll need to live on your own, in a house or apartment, away from the support structure of school or home.

Chances are you're looking for a job or already have one, and you're either ready to move into your own place or you already have moved and you're not sure you've got all your bases covered.

You know that mistakes can be costly, and you want to avoid making them!

You may already know some of the information in this book. That's okay—just go to the parts that are new to you. There's plenty within these pages to keep you busy.

We begin with the most basic life skill: knowing yourself. Of course, you're a complicated person and it's impossible to *completely* know yourself and what you want! But the better idea you have of who you are, the better your choices will be. Like every chapter, this first one concludes with a short section called *Take Action!*, which is a checklist of things you can do to help yourself move forward. The idea is that you can always *do something* to improve your life.

The second life skill is self-care. I mean this not only in the sense of keeping your body clean and healthy, but how to present yourself in public and at work. The rule is to dress *appropriately* for your job and to make people feel comfortable around you.

Then we tackle the subject of academic excellence. Whether in the classroom or in "the real world," the fundamental skill of learning is *reading*. If you can read well, you can continue to learn for the rest of your life. My *Take Action!* tips will help you keep improving yourself and thereby increasing your value in the job marketplace.

The fourth life skill is how to find and get hired for the job you want. This includes beginning with a summer job, understanding tax forms, and dealing with workplace challenges. I'll also share my "7 Tips for Succeeding at Your Job," and how to embrace neurodiversity at your place of employment.

Next is money management. I'll show you how to open a bank account, explore funds transfer apps, use credit cards to your advantage, and create a household budget—even if your "household" is just you and your cat! And who could forget income taxes, a fact of life that doesn't have to be painful.

Number six is all about paying for college. I'll reveal the ins and outs of the FAFSA form that just about every student and their family submits, and how you can take advantage of grants, scholarships, work-study programs, and federal loans.

The seventh life skill delves into transportation to work, school, and around town. You may take public transportation, ride a bike, walk, hire an Uber, or drive your own car—however you do it, I've got you covered!

Then we'll explore the secrets of getting your own place, which in all likelihood means renting an apartment. Roommate or no roommate? New or used furniture? And how about home security? It's all here, along with my *Take Action!* tips to give you specific ideas.

Life skill number nine is all about food. In this chapter we will discuss your experience and confidence in the kitchen and, should you have little of either, I'll offer some general advice and simple recipes you can learn in a flash. Eating a healthy diet is of course the ideal, but sometimes this ideal is difficult to reach. So we'll focus on the principle that *fed is best,* because eating enough of what is available to you is what matters the most.

I'll show you how to be a smart shopper, share some go-to sources for finding more recipes, and provide a rundown of the basic utensils and tools you'll need in your kitchen.

If you struggle financially, we'll also discuss shame-free, state-funded resources available to you for buying food.

Number ten is staying safe in both real and virtual worlds and protecting yourself against financial fraud. The goal isn't to scare you—no one wants to do that!—but to equip you with the knowledge and tools you need to live a happy and secure life on your own. When you live at home or in a college dorm, you've got other people around you, and there may be a security structure (in a college dorm, there should be!) Chance can bring you into many different living dynamics, with different kinds of people. Those who are strangers at first may eventually become friends. And having reliable, kind neighbors can be a boost. But strangers may remain exactly that. So whatever living situation you find yourself in, what is crucial to remember is that you are your priority and your responsibility, and you will need to take care of yourself. The same goes for your finances—you're earning your own money, have your own bank cards, and you need to know how to keep your cash safe.

Life skill number 11 is spirituality and morality, which go hand in hand to keep you on the right course in life. I'm not going to preach to you, but I can tell you that having a solid foundation in something bigger than yourself—whatever you call it—can help you weather life's many challenges and give your life greater meaning.

We have much to talk about! Ready? Let's get started!

1

Know Yourself

I am larger, better than I thought; I did not know I held
so much goodness.
All seems beautiful to me.
Whoever denies me, it shall not trouble me:
Whoever accepts me, he or she shall be blessed,
and shall bless me.

— Walt Whitman, *Leaves of Grass*

When you look in the mirror, whom do you see?
To make providing an answer easy, I'll give you some prefab choices. Don't think about it—just choose the one you're most comfortable with. Or even choose two or three! There are no rules here. No wrong answers.

Okay? Here we go:

When I look in the mirror, I see a person who is....

A. Confident and has a career goal.

B. Not sure what I want, but eager to try many different
   things in life.

C. Bewildered by the complexity of the world.

D. Totally dazed and confused.

E. Not interested in taking a stupid quiz.

Again, there are no correct answers. There's only you and who you are at this moment. Not last year, or when you were a little kid, or in the future.

Just right now.

I ask you this question because if you're capable of self-reflection and recognizing the person you are, you're already halfway to becoming a successful human being. If you know what you want from life—or even what you *don't* want—it's a million times easier to go out and get it, without wasting time.

That's why your ability to Know Yourself is the very first Actionable Life Skill.

Just for fun, let's say you know exactly your direction in life. Let's say you're like Bill Gates, who has had the same passion since he was around your age. He's a computer guy. Always has been, always will be. He even dropped out of college (Harvard!) to start his software business (Microsoft) at age 20.[3] And he made a ton of money by taking the road less traveled!

If this sounds like you, then I wish you every success. But stay open to new roads! Later in his life, Bill Gates, the computer geek, developed a profound interest in eradicating global infectious diseases.

But if certainty is good, or if you don't know what you want right now, are you doomed to failure?

Absolutely not!

The world is full of super-successful people who, had they taken my little quiz when they were still in school or just starting out, would happily have chosen D or E. They were not yet ready to say, "This is me. This is who I am." It took them a while. Their path in life was not clear. Well, that's okay. These people were able to look in the mirror and say, "Hello, there. Nice to meet you. I have no idea who you are and what you want."

It's perfectly alright to be restless and unsatisfied, and to have no clear ideas for your future. Lots of people have felt the same way. But eventually, even the people who have no direction and who don't know themselves have one thing in common:

They *do* something. They take *action*.

They don't just sit around and moan.

They say to themselves, "I don't know what I want, so I'm just going to try a bunch of stuff and see what I like. I'm going to learn about myself and the world."

That's the key! To succeed in life, we all need to keep learning and experiencing new things.

In fact, if there's just *one thing* I want you to take away from this book, it's this:

The minute you stop learning about yourself and the world,
you become like a compass without a needle:
unable to find any direction.

Life is change. Life is action. Life is growth. It's fine to not have a clear direction at first, as long as you're in motion.

I don't mean *literally* in motion. When you read a book, your body is at rest. It's your brain that's in motion!

I can hear some of you say, "How about meditation? Can't that be useful for learning about yourself?"

Yes, it can—in moderate doses. Nothing wrong with meditating! But unless you aspire to become a monk in a Buddhist monastery, you need to handle the practical aspects of life: earning money, supporting yourself, and finding your place in the world.

There's no greater satisfaction in life than being able to support yourself (and your family, if you have one) and being a contributing member of society. This is why, as you get older, you want to make the shift from being a *consumer* to being a *producer*.

Look at it this way: When you're a kid, you're strictly a consumer. You depend on adults to feed you, buy your clothes, and drive you around. The adults also tell you where you can go and what you can do. That's the tradeoff: You get protection and sustenance, and in return, you do what they want. Fair enough! But eventually—when you turn eighteen, or maybe twenty, or even later—you're ready to shift the equation. You're ready to get your own job, live in your own place, and go where you want to go. You want to make your own money and to do that, you must become a producer of something you can sell in the marketplace. You can do work, either for yourself or for an employer, and get paid.

The Public Me and the Private Me

As you read this book, one of the things I ask you to think about is the difference—if there is one—between the person you try to be in public versus the person you are when you're alone or around people you really trust.

Our goal is to narrow that gap, and for there to be just one all-purpose version of you. Why is that important? Because the wider the gap, the more *tension* you'll feel. If you're in public or with other people—even your own family—and you feel like you need to put on an act or pretend to be someone different than you really are, you will feel the internal stress. You may even want to say out loud, "Hey! This is the real me! Why can't you love me for the way I am?" By being the person other people want you to be, or even *demand* you to be, you may lose sight of who you really are.

I'm not talking about how you conduct yourself at work or in the classroom. In such environments, where everyone is expected to conform to "professional" levels of behavior so that the group can function productively, it's normal to adjust aspects of your behavior to get along with the demands of the organization. You might wear a nice suit to work, and then when you get home immediately change into ratty jeans and a t-shirt. That's perfectly fine!

Here, we're primarily talking about that dreaded phrase, "peer pressure." You're probably sick of hearing it, but it can be a significant force in your life. Peer pressure is the feeling that, for whatever reason, you must modify or adjust your behavior to be accepted by a group of people whom you want to join. In its simplest terms, it's like if everyone in your peer group—at school or community—wore yellow shirts. You like blue shirts, but you know you'll never be accepted by your peers unless you wear a yellow shirt too. So you swallow your pride and buy an ugly yellow shirt, and when you wear it, they accept you with open arms! Yay!

Many young adults are willing to do this because it's important for them to be part of the group. But what's incredibly annoying is when adults dismiss your feelings and say (for example), "Take off that hideous yellow shirt! Why are you wearing it? Oh—just because the other kids wear yellow shirts, then you think you have to? You should think for yourself!"

So now you've got your peers telling you, "Do this," while the adults are saying, "Do that."

And meanwhile, the adults all dress alike too! They conform to their peer group just as much as you do!

If you're getting the idea that there's no easy answer to this, you're right. In life, from time to time we all have to conform to the group. The question you should ask yourself is, "What am I getting in return? By *freely* making this choice, am I receiving a benefit?"

At the end of the day, what's important is that *you* are in charge of your life, and you have the confidence to choose how to live in both the personal and public worlds.

Finding Yourself Through Questioning

In the process of contemplating who you are and what you want from life, the journey can often feel overwhelming due to the mass of outside voices and expectations. Whether it's advice from parents, guardians, friends, teachers, or the influence of media and societal norms, the challenge lies in recognizing what truly aligns with your authentic self. Only by knowing this can you drown out the noise of conformity.

Self-awareness, the conscious knowledge and understanding of who you are as a person—including your feelings, thoughts, values, beliefs, emotions, motivations, and actions, is vital. Think of it as a mirror that helps you see and understand yourself as a whole.

Self-reflection is its essential companion, helping you figure out what values really matter to you, in an evolving process. It's through self-reflection that you can improve your self-awareness. Together, self-awareness and self-reflection serve as the starting point—placing your personal coordinates on a map.

Self-discovery is the adventure that guides you toward your dreams and goals—your destination—by exploring who you want to become and what you want to achieve.

This trio creates a roadmap to living in harmony with your true self, helping you make informed choices and navigate life's complexities.

Confused?

Fortunately, there is a time-honored method that simplifies the contemplation process by breaking it down into manageable components. It's commonly known as the 5WH (or 5W1H) method[4]—though I prefer the *5WH²*!

What? Why? Who? Where? When? How? And, How much?

If you've taken a journalism or writing class, this is probably familiar to you, except for the second "H," which I've added to address financial and budgetary questions—an essential part of managing your adult life.

The *5WH²* is an invaluable toolkit for your quest to better understand yourself and your aspirations. It's something you can rely on throughout your life when making decisions.

Here are examples of questions you can ask yourself to be more *self-aware*:

5WH²	Self-Awareness	Self-Discovery
	What are my personal interests and hobbies?	What do I want to achieve in my life?
	What are my strengths?	What are my areas for personal growth?
	What are my core values and beliefs?	What situations challenge my core values and beliefs?
What	What do I like? What do I not like?	What do I not want in my life?
	What makes me feel proud of myself?	What new achievements, qualities, and skills do I want to develop that will make me feel even prouder of myself?
	What makes me feel ashamed, and why?	What can I do to overcome the sources of shame in my life?

5WH²	Self-Awareness	Self-Discovery
Why	Why do I react the way I do in certain situations?	Why do I need to respond differently?
	Why do I have certain fears or insecurities?	Why do I need to overcome them?
	Why do I hold specific values and beliefs?	Why do I need to protect them from external pressures and influences?
	Why are the goals I've set for myself personally meaningful to me?	Why do I aspire to achieve them?
	Why do I want to improve or change certain aspects of myself?	Why do I feel the need to make these improvements or changes?
Who	Who are the people who influence me the most?	Who are the people who inspire me?
	Who can I turn to for support and guidance?	Who do I want to become in the future?
	Who are my closest friends and confidants?	Who can I rely on to help me achieve my goals and become a better version of myself?

5WH²	Self-Awareness	Self-Discovery
Where	Where do I feel most comfortable and at peace?	Where can I find the same peace when I move out?
	Where do I experience the most stress or anxiety?	Where do I see myself flourishing in the future?
	Where have I achieved significant milestones?	Where do I find inspiration and motivation that fit my goals?
When	When do I feel the most energized and motivated?	When can I consistently create conditions to feel the most motivated after I move out?
	When do I tend to procrastinate or lose focus?	When can I implement strategies to overcome procrastination and maintain focus more effectively?
	When do I feel lost?	When do I see myself feeling most grounded?

5WH²	Self-Awareness	Self-Discovery
How	How do I cope with stress and adversity?	How can I develop more effective strategies to improve my resilience?
	How do I communicate and interact with others?	How can I improve my communication skills to build more meaningful relationships?
	How do I make decisions and solve problems?	How can I improve my decision-making and problem-solving skills to align my actions with my goals and aspirations?
	How do I embrace change and personal growth?	How can I develop a mindset that welcomes change and supports my personal growth quest?
	How do I maintain a balance between self-care and productivity?	How can I create a daily routine incorporating self-care strategies without feeling guilty about my productivity?

5WH²	Self-Awareness	Self-Discovery
	How much time do I spend on self-reflection daily?	How much time and effort do I have to invest in pursuing my interests and passions?
	How much of my life is in alignment with my core values and beliefs?	How much progress do I need to make to ensure that the public image of myself reflects who I am in private?
How Much	How much do I earn and spend?	How much do I need to save and invest for my financial future?
	How much debt do I have, and why?	How much effort do I need to make to clear my debt and better manage my finances?
	How much do I value financial success and independence?	How much am I willing to adjust my financial habits to achieve my financial goals?

Practice asking these seven core *5WH²* questions as often as you can until it becomes second nature, and you'll find that many complex decisions suddenly become much simpler. You can also reference this in Appendix 2.

Growth Mindset Vs. Fixed Mindset

In 2007, a Stanford University psychologist named Carol Dweck published a book entitled Mindset: The New Psychology of Success.[5] In this book, she proposed the idea that people generally have one of two approaches to themselves and the world around them.

If you have what Dr. Dweck called a "growth mindset," this means that in a wide range of human experiences, you derive pleasure and satisfaction from learning new things, taking on new challenges, exploring the unknown, and—this is super important—risking being wrong. You're unfazed by mistakes and see them as learning opportunities. It's like when Thomas Edison was searching for the key to making the first practical light bulb; after yet another poor result, he said, "I have not failed. I've just found 10,000 ways that won't work." Obstacles are interesting challenges, not reasons to throw up your hands in surrender.

Having a growth mindset means not just the *capability* but the *desire* to expand your mind. It is a characteristic of people who want to seize as much from life as possible. To be a person who constantly evolves, regardless of circumstances, the growth mindset is essential. By weathering the good, the bad, and even the unexpected, and learning from it, you can reach your fullest potential. "If you have a brain, you want to learn because that's what the brain does,"[6] is a fitting encapsulation of the growth mindset, given by Canadian scientist, doctor, psychiatrist and neuroplasticity pioneer Norman Doidge, whose work we will consider further.

According to Dweck, to have the growth mindset is to believe that not only can you learn new facts, but you can elevate and improve your basic qualities as a human being. You can become more honest, more empathetic, and more articulate. You can learn leadership skills and strengthen your creative powers. With the sustained application of effort, you can transform yourself from a shy wallflower to a confident public speaker, or from someone who would rather follow to an inspirational leader.

The "fixed mindset" is quite different. This person feels as though they've got a well-defined set of capabilities, and these assets must be deployed to confirm that the person is of value. New ideas can be threatening because they represent an assault on what the person sees as their sacred self. An emerging new theory about some subject is greeted with suspicion. He or she is more likely to believe in fate, and accept setbacks as "what the universe wants." Tradition is important, as is the value of "eternal truths."

Before you jump to conclusions about yourself, please understand that this is not an either/or choice. These two approaches—growth and fixed mindset—exist on a spectrum, like wavelengths of light. Each one of us has aspects of both, and in different proportions. No one is purely one or the other.

We all need a solid foundation in proven facts and a belief in unchanging values. We all need to know that $2 + 2 = 4$, and that the Earth is round. These aspects of the fixed mindset are useful and positive.

But we also need to be curious about ourselves and our world. We need to take risks and innovate. Every advance made by human beings throughout history has been made because a person said, "What if?" and "How could this be better?" and "Let's create something new and beautiful." The essence of human life lies in the balance between the fixed mindset and the growth mindset.

By the way, the recognition of the growth mindset has a basis in emerging neurological science. For centuries, scientists believed that brain tissue—the billions of neurons and their connecting axons—could not be repaired if damaged, and did not change over time. This belief extended to thought patterns as well, and the notion that patterns or networks of thinking were unchangeable. In other words, the "operating system" of your brain could not be altered.

Then scientists developed the idea of *neuroplasticity*, the theory that the brain is a living, plastic organ, capable of near limitless change. With the term first used in 1948 by Polish neuroscientist Jerzy Konorski[7], neuroplasticity describes the ability of neural networks in the brain to change, through constant reorganization and rewiring.[8] Our brains are not hard-wired, like computers, a position Norman Doidge described as "spectacularly wrong."

Amazing strides have been made in the field of neuroplasticity over the past two-decades[9] by rejecting the 400-year-old "doctrine of the unchanging brain."[10] Through careful and rigorous therapy, neuroplasticity has been successful in treating trauma, depression, anxiety, autism, and learning disorders. By recognizing and annexing what the brain is already doing—constantly rewiring and restructuring itself—neuroplasticity successes have spilled over into the miraculous. There were cases of blind individuals gaining the ability to see, and one woman, born with half a brain, had her brain rewired to function as a whole.[11]

The main idea to understand about your brain is that your ability to think, feel, and make choices depends upon two things: your neurons (your brain cells) and the connections between them.

Scientists believe you have about 86 billion individual neurons in your brain.[12] In comparison, there are roughly 100 billion stars in our galaxy, the Milky Way, although we can't be certain—NASA places the high-end of the estimate at a mind-blowing 400 billion.[13]

While neurons can regenerate if damaged or diseased, it's unclear to what extent this can happen. Although an emerging area of science, the work of Doidge and others *has* shown that through brain exercises and neuroplasticity techniques, stroke patients have experienced improved outcomes. In one remarkable case, a 77-year-old man was able to reverse all of his Parkinson's disease symptoms.[14]

For your brain as an operating system, what really matters is that each neuron can make up to 1,000 *connections* with other neurons. This means your brain has about 60 trillion connections between all of your neurons. These connections are what allow you to think and feel, and remember and imagine. Here's the really amazing part: When grouped by their connections into packets or communities, your neurons can form nearly limitless *patterns*. It's these patterns of neurons that give you your unique personality. Over seven billion people live on this planet, and we all have the same biological brain with its 86 billion neurons.[15] If this is the case, then why are we not all identical, like robots? It's because our neurons can connect themselves in nearly infinite ways, giving each one of us a truly unique perspective on life.

Here's what's important for you: Today we know that while your neurons are relatively stable (perhaps they represent the fixed mindset!), the trillions of connections can change. They can be re-wired to form new pathways and relationships, and therefore new ways of thinking and even new habits. This is the growth mindset.

The ability to re-wire is most powerful when you're a kid or a young adult. Science has shown us that the male human brain is not fully developed until about age 25, and women achieve full brain development a bit earlier. So while your *body* may have reached the fully operational level by age 18—and you can do things like get a credit card or go to work full time—your *brain* takes longer to catch up.

The brain development that happens between 18 and 25 is a continuation of the process that starts around puberty, and at age 18, you're only about halfway through. Specifically, your prefrontal cortex is not yet fully developed. That's the part of the brain that handles impulse control (no surprise there!) and helps you make long-term plans.

In addition, right around the time of puberty, your brain's *reward system* becomes highly active, and then it gradually subsides to an adult level, which it reaches around age 25. As a teenager, you're more keenly aware of things like peer pressure because the disapproval of a peer makes a greater impact on your emotions. That's one reason why it can be super irritating when adults say things like, "He doesn't like you? Oh, just brush it off."

You're thinking, "How can this grown person be so *incredibly dense?*"

It's because the adult's brain is literally less sensitive than yours. They can't help it!

Adverse Childhood Experiences (ACEs)

While we're on the subject of annoying adults, it's very difficult when an old person says, "Just get your act together! Be a normal human being! What's your problem?" As if you can just magically snap your fingers and do everything right, all the time.

The fact is that you may have impulses and attitudes that you cannot control. "Self-discipline," which adults talk about so easily, can be monumentally difficult *even when your rational brain knows what you should do.*

How many times have you said to yourself, "I shouldn't do this," and yet you went ahead and did it anyway? You felt good for a short while, and then later on you felt guilty and embarrassed. You may have even gotten into trouble. And the adult says, "What were you thinking? Or were you not thinking at all?"

It happens all the time to many people just like you and me.

Here's the truth: Instead of demanding to know what you were *thinking*, the adult would have been more helpful if he or she had asked, "What were you *feeling* when you did that?"

That would have been a fair question. Feelings are strong and everybody has them. They don't always seem logical. They guide our actions as much as, or more, than thinking.

And guess what? Your brain controls both your thinking *and* your feelings.

So what can make your brain have strong feelings that you may not want or that bother you?

Part of the answer can be found in the *fight-or-flight response* that every person can experience.

When you feel threatened or scared, your body reacts by going into the fight-or-flight response. This can happen when you see a bear in the woods. It can also happen if an adult or other person hits you, you see alcoholism in your family, or you're physically or emotionally abused. In such moments, your body releases a flood of special hormones that changes your bodily functions. You breathe faster, your heart rate goes up, your stomach tightens, your hands get clammy. You prepare to fight, flee, or freeze.

When you see a bear, this response can help save your life!

Normally, when the danger is passed—the bear has walked away—your hormones subside. Your brain chemistry returns to normal. Your muscles relax and you stop perspiring. You can go on with your life.

When you're a child, any traumatic event that provokes a fight-or-flight response is called an *adverse childhood experience*, or ACE. The concept was developed in the late 1990s by the Centers for Disease Control and Prevention (CDC), an agency of the federal government, and Kaiser Permanente, an American integrated managed care consortium.[16]

To some degree, we've all had adverse childhood experiences—events that may be upsetting to us, like getting yelled at by an adult or getting into a fight with another kid. Ordinarily, if they are not too serious, they come and they go. They're not a lasting problem.

But what if you have lots of serious ACEs, all in a row, or repeatedly? What if you live in an abusive household or a dangerous neighborhood? Then you might have ACEs regularly. And each time you have one, your body goes into the fight-or-flight response. Hormones flood your brain over and over again. They never fully subside.

Why is that a problem? Because these hormones can *alter your brain chemistry*.[17] Your brain's operating system can become rewired to seek relief from the anxiety and stress that you feel on a daily basis. It can lead you to find comfort in behaviors that to others seem dangerous, including overeating, alcohol or drug abuse, and self-harming such as anorexia, hair pulling, and cutting. These behaviors appear bewildering to adults, but they may make you feel better for a short time.

If you have any of these feelings, please don't keep them a secret. Talk to a trusted adult or seek professional care. You can get help!

You can even take a short quiz to see if you're susceptible to the negative effects of ACEs. The confidential test—which is readily available online—is called the ACE quiz. Just Google "ACE quiz" and you'll find it on numerous legitimate websites. It's a short list of yes-or-no questions. It will take you about a minute to complete.

For example, the first question is, "Before your 18th birthday, did a parent or other adult in the household often or very often… swear at you, insult you, put you down, or humiliate you?"[18]

Yes or no?

There are more such questions.

The higher your ACE score, the greater your chances of suffering from psychological issues including chronic depression or self-harming, and even medical problems including cancer or coronary heart disease.

Again, while everyone has some memory of one or more adverse childhood events, if they are either particularly severe or repeated, they can alter your brain connections and make it more difficult for you to succeed at supporting yourself, staying healthy, and being happy.

To be sure, the ACE quiz is nothing more than a snapshot. It does *not* ask about the positive things in your life that could make an adverse experience easier to handle. It's strictly a tool to measure the likelihood that you may be burdened by a high ACE score. You may have a high ACE score and be a high-functioning person. Everyone is different!

If you have the slightest feeling that childhood trauma may be a factor in your life, talk to a trusted adult—parent, guardian, school counselor, coach, spiritual leader—or seek advice from a medical professional.

Talk to an adult you trust. It may seem scary and difficult, but give it a try.

You deserve every opportunity to succeed and be happy! The very first step toward a rewarding life is to know yourself and what you want to do in life. And for you, the most important task may be to explore your past and how it can influence your choices today.

TAKE ACTION!

- Think about what you really like to do. Without considering money, if you could occupy yourself with any activity, what would it be? No answer is too crazy. Be honest.

- Have you had any jobs yet, such as over the summer? Were they fun or just boring drudgery? Would you rather be in school or working at a job?

- Are you ready to plan your career, or do you want to try different things first? If you don't have a direction, then make a list of opportunities that might appeal to you. Do you like working with people, like in a restaurant or retail setting? Are you a creative person, and attracted to marketing? How about a career in STEM—that's science, technology, engineering, and mathematics? Ask your school guidance counselor for help in identifying jobs that would be a good fit for your skills.

- Use the $5WH^2$ method to better know yourself and align your actions with your personal goals and values. Begin by asking yourself "Who am I at my core, beyond societal roles and expectations?" and explore the other fundamental questions to help define your path in life.

- Looking back on your childhood, were there any traumatic incidents or episodes? Do you think they have any influence on your choices today?

- If you have a high ACE score, is there a trusted adult or healthcare professional to whom you can turn?

2

Self-Care

Our bodies are gardens, to the which our wills are gardeners.
— William Shakespeare, *Othello*

*A*long with our fellow humans, who currently number over seven billion, we live in the real, physical world. We're born, we grow, we do our thing, and if we're lucky—and take care of ourselves—we live to eighty or more years until, as Shakespeare said, we "shuffle off this mortal coil."

Each one of us gets one body to inhabit. It's issued to us at birth, and as newborns we have no choice in what we receive. All the things that make us who we are—our beautiful shade of skin, number of fingers and toes, our ability to smile and laugh—are the result of the DNA provided by our two biological parents.

Thanks, mom and dad!

In the very early years of life, we have little control over what happens to our bodies. We are strictly consumers, fed and clothed by our adult caregivers. If they provide healthy foods or processed junk food, it's not our choice. If they encourage us to exercise or just park us in front of a screen all day—again, as babies and little kids, we have little to say about it. Our caregivers take us to the doctor—hopefully—and teach us the fundamentals of good health, like brushing our teeth and washing our hands.

Gradually, as we get older, we gain more control over our bodies. At school, we can decide to play sports or join the computer club. We can buy our own snacks and choose our own beverages, and exert more authority over our food consumption at the dinner table. And as humans, we have the free will to ignore the law and experiment with illegal drugs and alcohol, even if it's against our best interests.

For many teens, going away to college and living in a dorm is the first time we're totally independent of our adult caregivers. Now we can eat whatever we want, whenever we want! Others get jobs and move away from home, or even if they continue to live at home, they have more autonomy.

The point is that gradually, over time, full responsibility for the body you've got falls into your hands.

It's *yours*. Not mom's or dad's, or grandma's, or some other caregiver.

All of the qualities you *like* about yourself are yours: Maybe it's your personality, your physical strength, or your beautiful hair.

And all of the qualities you *dislike* about yourself are yours too: Maybe it's your zits, your—as you perceive them—big ears, or your tendency to mumble when you talk. It may be something deeper, like your urge to cut yourself, your sickle cell anemia, or your diabetes.

All of it—the good and the bad—belongs to you.

As an adult, your body and mind are your responsibility and no one else's.

That's why Self-Care is the number two Actionable Life Skill. It's super important that you master it!

The question of good health may seem like a dumb topic to discuss because the answer is obvious: If you're in chronically poor health, you'll be sick more often and you'll likely die younger. People who are in good health, whether by sheer luck or their own effort, live longer and spend much less money on their own healthcare.

Adults, of course, are bewildered by the cavalier attitude many young people have about their physical well-being. This is because the bodies of adults take longer to heal when injured. If you're sixteen years old and you somehow manage to fall and break your hip (it's very rare for that to happen to a young adult), your bones will knit together quickly and you'll soon be back to normal. But if you're seventy years old and fall and break your hip, it could cripple you for life and trigger a cascade of other health problems.

Your Personal Health

You may have heard the old saying, "Without your health, you have nothing."

It's the truth! But healthcare is a hugely complicated subject, so we're going to oversimplify it by segmenting it into three categories.

1. Your Everyday Health Habits

These are the things you do daily to maintain good health, and over which you have full control. You brush your teeth, wash your face, take a shower or bath, use deodorant, shave if appropriate, pluck any weird little hairs growing where they shouldn't... You get the idea. You do the best you can with the body the universe and your biological parents gave you.

One of the keys to maintaining good health is to nourish your body with healthy foods and avoid junk foods. This is a topic we will discuss in full in life skill number nine. However, here are a few basics to note: drink lots of plain water, get plenty of restorative sleep, and exercise regularly.

A big concern these days is the presence of toxic or unhealthy ingredients in many of the everyday personal care products that we use, such as deodorants, lotions, and cosmetics. Not everyone has the time to research all the strange chemical names that appear on the long ingredients lists of these products and figure out which ones are safe and which are dangerous. Fortunately, there are apps for that! All you have to do is download an app such as Yuka, Think Dirty, or Detox Me. Point your phone at the barcode of the product you're considering and *voilà!* The app will explain the ingredients and provide a safety rating. Every app works a bit differently, so it's worth trying them out to see which one works best for you.

For now, let's talk about diet in general, and some social issues surrounding it. You probably know that one of the most serious health issues facing not just young people but adults worldwide is excess body weight and obesity.

Recent reports by the World Obesity Project predict, in the next 12 years, over 51 percent of the global population will be obese or overweight. That's over 4 billion people, and the figure includes children.[19] Weight can be a sensitive subject to address for two reasons:

1. Being overweight or obese may contribute to serious lifelong diseases including diabetes.
2. "Fat shaming" is not cool and no one should be made fun of because of their weight or appearance.

These two facts can seem to contradict each other! The truth is that how much your body wants to weigh (that is, how much body fat it wants to store up) is a super-complicated issue with few clear answers. Some people have bodies that relentlessly store extra calories as fat, while other people don't. If you are happy with your body weight, then be happy! Celebrate it! But if you want to lose weight, there are countless methods and programs available. Ask your doctor, school nutritionist, or a registered dietician for guidance.

Another challenge facing young people is the easy availability of both illegal and prescription narcotics. Do not take *any* drug or pill unless you know exactly what's in it and why you're taking it. In particular, fentanyl is a *killer*. According to the Centers for Disease Control and Prevention (CDC), in the 12-month period ending in January 2022, over 100,000 people in the United States died of drug overdoses and drug poisonings—and 67 percent of those deaths involved synthetic opioids, including fentanyl. This is very bad stuff!

These are all things that you can control—and they make a huge difference.

2.   Diseases and Accidents

We live in a world where we're all subject to the forces of nature. We get sick and have accidents that require professional care. Fortunately, young people tend to have fewer serious health issues than older people, but they also have an idealized view of their own mortality.

The bottom line is this: When you're really sick, go to the doctor! Don't put it off. Don't try to "power through" what could be a serious illness.

Of course, depending on the state you live in, your educational level, and your life experience, your awareness of the availability and cost of healthcare will vary. The American healthcare system is largely privatized and highly fragmented. Your access to covered healthcare will depend on many factors including what kind of health insurance plan you have. Under the Affordable Care Act, you may be covered under your parents' or guardians' health plan. If you work, you may have a health plan through your employer. If you're not sure, go online to your state government website and find out, or Google the Affordable Care Act.

If you are seriously ill, bleeding, or are in pain, do not hesitate to go to the nearest emergency room. Your health is too important to be timid! Get medical attention quickly, and sort out the details later.

3. Chronic Diseases with a Psychological Basis

Remember the discussion about Adverse Childhood Experiences (ACEs)? Many young people suffer from mysterious conditions that seem to control their behavior and which may be deeply rooted in childhood. They include eating disorders such as anorexia and bulimia, cutting, pica (eating non-food items), and trichotillomania (pulling one's hair). Obesity can also be caused by childhood trauma, as can suicidal ideation. And of course, there's smoking cigarettes and excessive alcohol and drug consumption.

These stubborn and harmful conditions usually require professional help to resolve. If you experience any of them, talk to your parent or guardian, school counselor, healthcare provider, or spiritual advisor for advice on how to receive treatment. It's your body and your life—don't let past experiences that were beyond your control deprive you of your health and freedom!

Meditation, Mindfulness, and Restorative Sleep

Many people of all ages find confidence, comfort, and support through the practice of meditation, mindfulness, or both.

Meditation is the practice of looking inward and often focusing on one thought or bodily process, such as breathing. It usually requires a defined time and space, and is a specific activity that we intentionally pursue in our everyday lives.

Meditation can have a noticeable effect on a part of your brain called the amygdala, which is part of our survival mechanism. It's designed to respond when it senses a "trigger" or any information that it perceives as threatening. In teens, the amygdala is very sensitive and can react strongly to things like being criticized by a peer or seeing an embarrassing social media post about yourself. Meditation can help you calm your amygdala and your overall emergency response, lower your fight-or-flight response, and let you see problems from a more manageable perspective.

Mindfulness is different. Instead of focusing inward, it's a state of active, open attention to the present moment. It's about keenly *observing* your thoughts and feelings without judging them as painful or pleasant. It's like you're watching a movie about your feelings. You know they exist, but they don't affect your heart rate or your breathing. But this high level of awareness will prompt you to make conscious choices based on what you're experiencing.

The practice of mindfulness is not religious. While it derives from ancient traditions of Eastern religious and spiritual institutions, including Buddhism and Hinduism, elements are also found in Judaism, Christianity, and Islam, and it's become a secular practice around the world from which anyone can benefit.

You can practice mindfulness in any situation at any time. While you simply walk around during the day, use your five senses to notice the temperature, the sounds in your environment, the people around you, the smell of the air, the feeling of the breeze brushing your cheeks, and how your body feels as it moves.

While eating, instead of just "chowing down," be aware of your food and how it provides nutrition for your body. In a group, be aware of anyone who feels left out (this requires empathy, a very important personal attribute for anyone).

When you're on a date, be aware of where you are, what your partner may want or *not* want from you, how much you're drinking, and whether you are truly *choosing* to do whatever you're doing. Know when you're supposed to go home—and how you're going to get there. Before you get into a car, be aware if the driver has been drinking or is high—and be prepared to refuse to go along.

Both meditation and mindfulness work to hold us responsible and accountable for our thoughts. They demand we sharpen our skills of focus and concentration, and improve our self-awareness. They help us find inner peace and relax our bodies, and can be done just about anywhere and anytime.

They can supplement your regular efforts to maintain a healthy body and clear mind—and even better, they cost you nothing!

Now, let's talk about sleep.

Did you know that the advantages derived from sleep depend not only on the duration you spend in bed, but also on the *quality* of your sleep?

Sleep is intended to be restorative and recharge your brain for the next day, but if it's interrupted, it's not going to meet that goal. When you sleep at night, your brain should cycle through four distinct stages.[20]

Stage 1: This is when you're just falling asleep. Called "light sleep," it can last for 1-5 minutes. If you awaken during this period, you may not even be aware you dozed off.

Stage 2: "Deeper sleep" lasts about 25 minutes. As your heart rate slows, your body temperature drops. By now you are fully asleep and unaware of your surroundings[21]. Scientists believe you may also be consolidating and sorting memories from the day. The annoying habit of teeth-grinding (bruxism) *can* occur at this stage.

Stage 3: "Deepest Sleep" lasts for 30 minutes to an hour. Even loud environmental noises or activity may fail to wake you during deep sleep. If you *do* wake up, you will feel woozy and your brain functioning will be impaired for 30 minutes to an hour. This stage is crucial for strengthening the immune system, tissue regrowth, and building bone and muscle. It's linked with the development of insightful thinking, creativity, and further memory consolidation. It's the true "restorative sleep."[22] But because your body and mind are so relaxed, it *can* come with the potential downsides of sleepwalking, bed wetting, and night terrors.

Stage 4: This is known as REM sleep (yes, just like the famous rock band from the 1980s!). REM stands for "rapid eye movement." While the rest of your body is immobilized, your brain is highly active and your eyes twitch as you experience vivid dreams. During REM sleep, your brain activity resembles being awake, and you may even wake suddenly. REM sleep is vital for various cognitive functions, yet it's not considered restorative. Just as it enables dreams, nightmares can occur during this stage as well. In general terms, REM sleep will first occur at around 90 minutes after you fall asleep. The first of these REM sleep stages lasts around 10 minutes, building gradually throughout the night to a peak of one hour.

A complete sleep cycle through all four stages lasts about 80 to 100 minutes and then repeats again, several times, during the night. Every night, you need to get enough sleep to cycle repeatedly through all four stages, with the average standing between 4 to 6 times.[23]

How about you? Do you get enough *quality* sleep? Maybe you stay up too late and feel like you have to get up too early, especially on school days?

If you're sleep deprived, it's not your imagination.

Researchers say that teens and young adults actually need more sleep than children—at least nine hours a night for optimum health. A 2010 large-scale study published in *The Journal of Adolescent Health* found that less than 8 percent of U.S. high school students get the recommended amount of sleep on school nights.[24]

According to a 2006 National Sleep Foundation poll, more than 87 percent of high school students in the United States get far less than the CDC-recommended 8 to 10 hours.[25] More alarming is the fact that the amount of time they sleep is decreasing. Sleep deprivation increases the likelihood of negative effects including an inability to concentrate, anxiety, depression, poor grades, drowsy-driving incidents, and even thoughts of suicide and suicide attempts.[26]

Sleep deprivation can put young people into a chronic mental fog, said Mary Carskadon, PhD, a professor of psychiatry at Brown University and director of chronobiology and sleep research at Bradley Hospital in Rhode Island. "One of the metaphors I use is that it's like having an astigmatism. You don't realize how bad your vision is until you get glasses or in this case, good sleep." That haze, according to Dr. Carskadon, writing for the *Child Mind Institute*, can negatively affect your emotions and mood, and impact your ability to think, react, regulate your emotions, learn in school, and get along with others.[27]

What are the causes of sleep deprivation among young people, according to the *Child Mind Institute*? They include:

1. Early school starting hours—sometimes as early as 7:30 AM.
2. Your own hormones, which may conspire to keep you awake long past the time when you should be asleep. This is particularly true if you are a "night owl."
3. Overscheduling of extracurricular activities.
4. Demands of homework at night.
5. Nighttime screen time.
6. Caffeine.

Unfortunately, factors 1 and 2 are out of your control. You just have to manage them as best as you can, and try not to worry. If you feel like the stress is too much, don't be afraid to consult your primary care physician, parents, or guardians. Sleep deprivation can lead to depression, anxiety conditions, and even substance abuse—it's serious business.[28]

Factors 3 and 4 are ones you can talk to your parents or guardians about. Both extracurricular activities and the demands of hefty homework are often felt to be obligatory elements to securing top college spots. As *Stanford Medicine* notes, students often face four to five hours of homework after an already long day in the classroom, and will often push themselves until they collapse. But sleep is vital for daytime functioning and actually helps with memory consolidation and learning. So taking tests while sleep-deprived is unlikely to result in good grades.[29]

Regarding homework, try not to procrastinate. And if you feel like you have a tendency to do so, consider talking to a guidance counselor who may be able to help you plan your time and set concrete goals.

Above all, remember that, as *Stanford Medicine News Center* puts it, sleep is as important for your well-being as exercise and nutrition. It is anything but "unproductive."

Factors 5 and 6 are things over which *you* have absolute control. Every sleep doctor on the planet will tell you (and every adult) that you must shut off all screens and electronic devices well before bedtime.[30] *Do not take your phone to bed with you.* If you use your phone as an alarm clock, then buy yourself an old-fashioned alarm clock. Leave your phone outside your room.

As for caffeinated beverages, they're quite simply a fact of life. You don't get enough sleep, so you have a coffee or energy drink. This, in turn, can contribute to not being able to fall asleep when night time rolls around, requiring more caffeine the next day. It's a vicious cycle, but it can be broken! Despite societal acceptance, it's important to remember that caffeine *is* technically a drug. Side effects can include high blood pressure, increased heart rate, headaches, anxiety, dehydration, hyperactivity, poor sleep, and irritability. If you must drink caffeine, remember to do so in moderation.

A recent study in the *Journal of Clinical Sleep Medicine*[31] found that consuming 400mg of caffeine—the equivalent of 4 cups of coffee, 10 cans of cola, or two "energy shot" drinks[32]— within 6 hours before bedtime can seriously disrupt your sleep, causing more awakenings, reducing total sleep time, and lowering sleep quality. Repeating this "sleep-debt" pattern over multiple nights can negatively impact your daytime functioning. So, to ensure restorative sleep, pay attention to your sleep hygiene.

As a general guideline, avoid caffeinated drinks (including non-herbal teas and caffeinated sodas!) at least eight hours before bedtime.

You can use apps like HiCoffee, EveryDrink, or Cup Buddy to help monitor your caffeine intake.

One last piece of advice, drawn from my personal experiences, is about chugging water right before bed. It may seem healthy, but it can disrupt your precious sleep by increasing nighttime awakenings, for bathroom use. That's why Dr. Conroy, a behavioral sleep expert, recommends limiting your intake to less than 12 ounces in the couple of hours before bedtime.[33] A better strategy is to stay well-hydrated earlier in the day, instead of trying to catch up on water intake during the evening.

The bottom line is that you cannot do it all! Try to be disciplined and get the restorative sleep you need. Your body will thank you, especially your brain!

Presenting Yourself to Other People

Aside from the personal longevity benefits of taking care of your health, the other aspect—which is important to everyone, regardless of age—is that unless you plan to live like a hermit, alone in the woods, then your life will include regular and meaningful contact with other human beings. Many of these people will be in a position to make your life better by hiring you, buying your product or service, or working in partnership with you. These people—employers, customers, colleagues—*will judge you according to your appearance and behavior.*

That may seem unfair, but it's reality.

We've talked about how few choices you have as a kid. You go where your caregivers take you, and even your friends are often determined not by your choice but by who happens to be in your class, on your team, or living in your neighborhood. Some random kid moves in next door, and he or she is now to be treated as a friend, whether you like it or not.

As you get older, *you* have more choices, and so do the employers, customers, and colleagues with whom you interact.

An employer advertises for a new employee, and he or she will get ten, twenty, or even more applications from qualified candidates just like you. The person hiring—whether she's the manager at your corner Burger King or the vice president of human resources at a Wall Street financial firm—will choose the candidate who she thinks is the *best fit for the company*. The choice will be made according to your resume and work history, qualifications, the job interview, and—very important!—your personal appearance and behavior.

Customers buy services—house cleaning, insurance, estate planning—based on the same criteria, as will anyone with whom you might go into business. In every case, your appearance will be used as an indicator that you're the right person for the job, contract, or partnership.

It's true that you have the right to refuse to "play the game," just as you can choose to stay at home or in your cabin in the woods. You also have the right to be broke and live in poverty, if that's what you want. I assume that's not what you want. You want to be a success in life, which means playing the game.

But it's not as onerous as it may sound. You should want to appear clean and well dressed, but as far as your mode of dress is concerned, you should always *dress appropriately for the job*.

This means your appearance should match the opportunity.

Are you applying for a position as a software coder? Clean and neat casual attire is what you want.

Bank teller? A button-down shirt and tie for guys, neat office attire for women.

Landscaper? Rugged boots, jeans, and a flannel shirt.

DJ at the local club? You'd better look trendy! Blue hair might work, and a leather jacket.

Can you imagine someone showing up at a job interview for a garage mechanic wearing a business suit? Crazy, right? Or someone in mechanics overalls and combat boots applying for a job as a high school math teacher? Not going to happen!

When organizing yourself for work, be empathetic. This means being considerate of the feelings of others and the quality of their experience with you. Here, details matter, especially when it's your personal hygiene. One of the top reasons hiring managers reject otherwise qualified applicants is poor personal hygiene: body odor (BO), dirty fingernails, bad breath. Body odor in particular is offensive because it *invades the other person's space*. You cannot escape it, especially if you're sharing a cubicle or a small office or storefront. The same applies to strong perfumes and colognes. If you're a guy, it may be cool to drench yourself in Axe Body Spray when you head out to the club on a Friday night, but it's not cool to show up at work reeking of it. Don't forget you need to be clean, smell neutral, brush your teeth, trim your nails. Be the person others want to be around!

And how about those pesky body and facial hairs that you want to get rid of? In the old days you had to shave them, use wax, or pluck them. Ouch! Today, you have another option—intense pulsed light (IPL) technology. These devices use strong pulses of light to heat and disable the roots of hairs, causing the hair to fall out, often permanently. Results will vary, and it may take a few applications to work. There may be some skin sensitivity, and experts caution that people with diabetes and certain other conditions should not use them. Be sure to read the directions carefully, and if you have questions, talk to your dermatologist—but who knows, IPL might be just what you need for smooth skin!

Dress Sense

Along with the willingness to dress appropriately for the role you want—which shouldn't be much of a burden because if you want a particular job, it stands to reason that you want to be a part of that world and be accepted by it—there's also what we call "dress sense." It's simply the ability to dress in combinations of clothes that look good on you and are flattering. Now this can be a matter of taste, but once again, we're talking about your willingness to play the game and follow the accepted customs of the current culture. Dress sense does not necessarily refer just to what *you* think looks good on you, but what the *other person* is likely to think looks good on you *for the occasion.*

Here's an example. Sally is getting ready for a job interview at the office of a local mortgage broker. She goes to her closet and picks out a pair of jeans and a sweatshirt.

Her friend Seth comes over. He sees Sally is getting ready.

"Are you going out?" he asks.

"Yes, to a job interview," she replies. "At First National Mortgage. I'm going to be a mortgage officer."

Seth frowns. "In jeans and a sweatshirt? Really? Don't you think you should be wearing the appropriate attire? Your current job is with a trendy marketing company, where it's cool to wear casual clothes to work every day. But a financial services company is very different. The dress code is more traditional business. If you're going to enter that industry, you need some dress sense!"

Again, no one is saying that Sally can't wear her jeans and sweat-shirt, or that she doesn't look terrific in them. But if she wants to work in an office that has a conservative image, she needs to dress the part.

Where can you find out more about dress sense?

You can learn it where you can learn just about anything else, of course—online! Just go to your phone or desktop, Google "learn dress sense for work," and you'll find a host of websites and YouTube videos that can help you.

Here's another way: If you're applying for a job and you can either visit the actual job site or get information online, then when you go for an interview, just *dress as though you already worked there.* Wear the same style of clothing as other people are in the position you want.

If you have limited access to the appropriate attire for the job you want, especially if it's in an office environment, check your area for charitable agencies that assist people in your position. For example, Dress for Success is a worldwide not-for-profit organization that helps women in many areas of professional excellence including support with professional attire. Other organizations that can help you look sharp for your interview are Jails to Jobs and Project Smile. Just Google the phrase "Charity provides work clothing" and you'll see the results in your area.

When dressing for a job interview or for work, do not try to express your individuality, unless that's what is expected. Don't just look at what the other employees are literally wearing; try to get a feel for the vibe of the company culture.

You're just going to have to use your common sense.

TAKE ACTION!

- Ask yourself what you usually wear: 1) around the house, 2) when you're out or at school, and 3) to your job, if you have one. Are they the same, or different? And how do you feel about that?

- Do you know how to present yourself for a job interview? Find out what the normal dress code is where you want to apply, and ensure your outfit will be appropriate for work.

- Do you have a good dress sense? You should develop a sense of what looks good on you balanced against what you need to wear to go to work.

- How would you characterize your physical health? If you have any issues you want to target, write them down and construct a plan for addressing them. See a healthcare professional before making any big decisions.

- If you have a disorder or bad habit that may have psychological roots, or you cannot solve it on your own, do not hesitate to talk to a *trusted* adult who can help you get the therapy you need. You deserve to lead a happy, productive life!

3

Ace Academics

The future depends on what we do in the present.

— Mahatma Gandhi

A ce Academics is the third Actionable Life Skill. It's all about gaining the knowledge you need to succeed in life within a school setting. Of course, there are many ways to learn about the world that are valuable, but there's no substitute for earning your high school diploma and then going to college and even graduate school.

As you'll recall, we started the first chapter of this book with a short quiz. The question was about who you saw in the mirror. There were no "wrong" answers, only the answers that worked for you.

Since this chapter is about school, it seems appropriate that it, too, should begin with a pop quiz. There are five statements. Choose as many as reflect how you feel right now, without concern over being "right" or "wrong."

Here goes:

When I think about going to school every day, I'm...
A. Happy because I really like my school.
B. Feeling mixed emotions. I like parts of it and don't like other parts.

C. Nervous because it's difficult for me.

D. Totally dazed and confused. I don't understand why I have to go.

E. Ready to get out as soon as possible to get a real job and make money.

You're entitled to feel however you like! School is a very specific type of environment— some love it and some don't. But there are some basic facts about formal education that you must know and be clear about.

First of all, in every state in the US, school attendance is required by law until a certain age. Every state sets its own age requirement: some are as low as 16, while others are as high as 18. So until you reach the minimum age in your state, you need to show up and try to do the work. There are a few exceptions, most notably if your parents or guardians are teaching you through an approved homeschooling program.

Also, if you don't earn your high school diploma in a classroom, you can get your GED, which is shorthand for the General Educational Development test. This is a group of four academic subject tests, and if you pass, you're certified as having United States high school-level academic skills.

You may notice that the vast majority of entry-level jobs require either a high school diploma or a GED. That's the absolute bare minimum. Why does it matter? Because without a high school diploma, you're going to be stuck at the very bottom of the economic barrel for your entire life. You will be virtually unemployable.

That's no joke. The US Bureau of Labor Statistics reports on the average earnings of people at various stages of educational accomplishment. Here are the BLS numbers as of 2021:

EDUCATION LEVEL	MEDIAN USUAL WEEKLY EARNINGS
Doctoral degree	$1,909
Professional degree	$1,924
Master's degree	$1,574
Bachelor's degree	$1,334
Associate's degree	$963
Some college, no degree	$899
High school or GED	$809
No high school or GED	$626

You can see a very simple and clear correlation: The biggest jump in pay is from no high school to having a high school diploma or GED. The more formal schooling you have, the more money you're going to make. It's a no-brainer.[34]

There are some additional facts that you may already know and should be acknowledged.

To become a professional, such as a doctor, dentist, lawyer, or mechanical or electrical engineer, you must complete the required formal education process for your chosen profession. There are no shortcuts and no substitutes. For example, to become a practicing physician in the US, you first need to earn your four-year undergraduate degree, typically majoring in a scientific or "pre-med" field. Then you must complete an accredited medical school program, which takes four years, and then at least three years of residency training before being able to practice independently. Each state may have its own additional requirements, including an exam and other training.

If you want to enter a trade, such as being a plumber or electrician, you need to follow a rigorous program of education and then pass a written and practical exam to get your license.

On the other hand, if you want to be a self-employed entrepreneur, you can start a business at any age. You may have heard about Sir Richard Branson, who began his business career at age 16 by founding a magazine called *Student*. He then went on to open a chain of record stores—the Virgin Group—and then he started a music label, an airline, and in 2021, realized a 17-year long dream by taking off in a test flight to outer space in his Virgin Galactic rocket ship.[35] If you think Elon Musk is impressive, then you'd be interested to know that in June 2023, Sir Richard created an entirely new industry—space tourism. For $450,000, the world's wealthy can now enjoy a 90-minute jaunt that is literally out of this world. This is entrepreneurship at a truly interstellar level, and today, Branson is not only one of the wealthiest people in the world, he's made history.[36]

So what does Sir Richard Branson, who never went to college, have in common with the most highly educated people in the world?

They all have a relentless drive to *learn*. No matter how they do it—whether in a classroom or on the job—they have a *growth mindset*. We talked about this in the first chapter. A growth mindset is focused on learning and then putting that knowledge to use to improve not only your life but the lives of other people. So while going to school is an effective, structured way to learn what you need to, at the end of the day, it's up to you to keep learning and building your skill sets.

Reading: The Fundamental Building Block of Learning

The number one academic skill that can change your life is your ability and desire to read. It is fundamental. To succeed in school, you must be a good reader; and if you're a good reader, you can continue your learning anyplace, anytime. The knowledge of the world will be at your fingertips.

Hopefully, your journey into reading began at a young age, when you were a toddler. Many parents and guardians enjoy reading story-books to their children. This instills a love of books, opens minds to new ideas, ignites the imagination, and begins the process of acquiring reading skills. Then you're introduced to reading and writing at school, and you learn the alphabet by singing your ABCs. Your first books are simple board books, then picture books. When you're aged seven to nine you start reading chapter books, which have anywhere from 4,000 to 15,000 words. From there, you graduate to easy readers, then young adults, and then regular adult books.

Do you have a favorite book from childhood? I hope so!

But perhaps you don't. Perhaps where you grew up, reading was not considered to be important, and as a child you didn't learn to read very well. That's okay! The wonderful thing about reading and writing is that you can learn at any age, and you can always improve.

Consider the true story of a woman who learned to read and write when she was over a century old.

In 1848, Mary Hardaway Walker was born into a family of en-slaved people in Union Springs, Arkansas. She was taught neither read-ing nor writing. In 1863, at age 15, she became a free person, and by age 20, she was married and had her first child. She and her family moved to Chattanooga, Tennessee, where she did various jobs including cleaning, cooking, providing childcare, and selling sandwiches for her church.

As the years and decades passed, she didn't know how to read or write.

By 1963, she was 115 years old. Her husband and children had passed away. Then she made the decision to learn how to read and write. She enrolled in a class offered by the Chattanooga Area Literacy Movement (CALM), where she was taught by a volunteer teacher named Helen Kelly. For more than a year, Mary attended a one-hour class two nights a week, where she learned to read, write, add, and subtract. Her story caught the attention of the public, and she received accolades from many Federal and local agencies and dignitaries. At age 121, she passed away, having, for a brief but wonderful period of years, enjoyed the pleasure and benefits of reading.[37]

Mary Walker had a growth mindset that flourished late in life! It's never too late to improve yourself and reach for a better tomorrow.

How can you improve your reading?

The most obvious way is to do what Mary Walker did, and enroll in a class in your community. But perhaps you're working or for some reason can't attend a class. That's no problem! The great thing about reading is that the more you do it, the better you get at it. The key is to read what you really love. They could be novels, historical books, memoirs, or self-help books, like the one you're reading now. Or you can read newspapers or magazines online, or trade magazines that relate to your job or career. Most mass-market books and periodicals are written using very basic English, but if you read technical books or literary novels you'll be exposed to new words. Having a free dictionary app handy, such as the authoritative Merriam-Webster, will help you expand your vocabulary quickly and infinitely!

If reading is a problem and you're struggling, you may have a reading disorder. Dyslexia is a common type of reading disorder. While it varies from person to person, common characteristics are difficulty with spelling, phonological processing (the manipulation of sounds), and rapid visual-verbal responding. Basically, it makes reading very difficult.

Having dyslexia can be embarrassing, but many very successful people have dealt with it. The famous entertainer Whoopi Goldberg said that when she discovered her difficulties in reading stemmed from her dyslexia, she was relieved. "It was nice to know I wasn't just lazy and that I didn't have to explain to people anymore that it wasn't that I didn't want to [read], it's just that I was having a hard time... The thing that crushed me more than anything was I didn't understand how they didn't see I was smart, I just couldn't figure things the way they were doing it."[38]

Treatment for dyslexia focuses on the specific learning problems of affected individuals. People with dyslexia develop a toolkit of coping strategies, and repeatedly drilling information helps a dyslexic student feel more confident, leading to enhanced performance over time. If you struggle to read, be sure to talk to your teacher, counselor, caregiver, or other *trusted* adult.

Please do not rely on social media videos and posts for your information about the world. Read news reports from trusted, major sources that have processes in place to check facts and verify the truthfulness of reports. Remember to use $5WH^2$ to verify your news sources!

If English isn't your native language, you may have trouble understanding the teacher in class and completing your work. Your school probably offers classes in English as a Second Language (ESL). These classes can help anyone learn English speaking, reading, and writing skills. They're also useful for employees who need specific English skills for their field, or college students or employees who need to pass English language tests to pursue advanced education. If you're seeking to advance your career in business, your English language skills are incredibly important. It's possible to work at an entry-level job in a restaurant, landscaping company, or on a farm with minimal English language skills, but you want to move up in the world, don't you? To elevate yourself, earn more money, and have a more fulfilling life, practice your English speaking and writing skills so that you can talk to anyone in any position!

Textbooks, Lectures, and Notes

Textbooks are designed to convey information to you in a neutral and non-judgmental way. This is the definition of *expository* writing. This is in contrast to *descriptive* writing (more colorful, like product descriptions), *persuasive* writing (designed to make you believe a certain point of view), and *narrative* writing (telling a story.)

The goal is to read, comprehend, and remember as much as possible about the subject being discussed. There are specific methods of reading that can help you do it better.

The SQRRR or SQ3R method can boost reading comprehension. Introduced by Francis P. Robinson, an American education philosopher, in his 1946 book *Effective Study*,[39] it's named for its five steps: survey, question, read, recite, and review.

Created for college students, it's useful for anyone. Here are the five steps.

Survey (S). The first step, survey (or skim or scan), advises that you should begin by reading the introduction before skimming through the chapters and noting the headings, sub-headings, and other visible features including graphs, tables, figures, or illustrations. This survey step takes only a few minutes but provides the "30,000-foot view" of the chapter you need to read.

Question (Q). Here, you make questions about the content of the reading. You do this by converting headings and subheadings into questions. Then you search for the answers in the content of the text. Other more general questions may also be asked, such as "What questions does this chapter answer?"

Read (R1). Next, you fill in the information around the book's structures you've been building in your mind. Start on page one and read carefully, while keeping in mind the questions to which you're seeking answers. This is called *active reading*.

Recite (R2). Try to recite from memory what you've learned, just as if you were telling someone else about the information. Don't just memorize the words and recite them; report on the contents using your own words as much as possible. This recital step may be either spoken or written, and enhances your ability to retrieve the material at a later date, such as for a test.

Review (R3). Once you reach the end of the chapter or section, review the material by repeating back to yourself the essential meaning of the passage. Again, this is not an exercise in memorization; put the thoughts into your own words.

This system can help you efficiently read a textbook and retain as much of it as possible without feeling as though you're cramming!

A similar system can be used for taking notes during a lecture. Since the speaker is probably not going to stop, especially in a big lecture hall, you need to be fast and efficient.

The key is to jot down the most important concepts of the information being given to you. These notes are meant to jog your memory, not provide a detailed record of every word said.

As you listen, use keywords and phrases instead of full sentences —almost like writing in shorthand. Organize your notes into a logical list of key ideas. If it's more convenient, use bulleted and numbered lists to expand on them more easily.

Conquering Boredom

It would be wonderful if every minute of every day at school were interesting and exciting, and you never felt bored. The reality is that in high school and even college, you're going to be taking some required classes that may not be interesting to you. You may like art and music and wonder why you're being forced to sit through a trigonometry class; or you may be a pre-med student and find yourself dozing off during your Victorian literature seminar.

This happens to every student once in a while. There can be two reasons why you may find yourself bored in class:

1. The subject matter doesn't interest you. You don't see the value in studying it. You ask yourself, "Why am I here? This is not relevant to my life. I want to learn—but I don't want to learn *this*."

   Every subject has value if you can see it. You can be brave and ask to speak to your teacher or counselor, and say to him or her, "Can you please show me why I should care about this subject? You see, I'm interested in ___ and ___, and I just don't get the connection." Teachers love the subjects they teach, and your teacher will be happy to try to get you more excited about it.

2. You might like the subject matter, but the teacher is boring. Maybe he or she drones on in a monotone, making you sleepy. While we're taught to respect our teachers, let's face it, they're human, and some are more engaging than others. In this case, you've just got to give your teacher a break. Learn the material, earn the very best grade you can, and get on with your life.

3. The class is too easy for you. If this is the case, and getting straight A's is not a challenge, talk to your teacher or counselor about getting access to higher level courses.

Are you bored during a required course? Then there's not much you can do except try to find a way to ignite your curiosity for it. Are you bored during an elective course that *you have chosen*? Then either change courses or, if it's too late to do that, perhaps you could volunteer to tutor other students or help teach the class!

Outside of school, in your life, boredom should be seen as an opportunity to *learn something new*. Being bored for a protracted period of time simply means that you don't feel challenged and you have no goal toward which you're striving. You're treading water. When you feel bored, ask yourself, "Have I set a goal for myself? Am I satisfied with life? Have I accomplished everything I've set out to do? Do I know everything there is to know?"

I hope your answer is a resounding "No! I have so much more to do and learn!"

When you're feeling bored, take it as a sign you need to kick-start your brain! Think about what will spark your interest. Perhaps you could set a new goal for yourself. Start a project. Read a new book. Go somewhere you've never been before. Visit an art museum. Call an old friend.

Whatever you do, try to avoid going shopping. Shopping as a cure for boredom is expensive and not very effective!

Academic Ethics

You know how easy it can be to cheat on a test or an assignment.

You can buy a term paper online for just a few dollars. You can even use AI to write one for you. You can look up answers on a smartphone, keep notes on a calculator, or listen to prerecorded solutions on an MP3 player. There are endless ways to "game the system" and turn in a piece of work that you didn't write, and think you're going to get an easy A grade.

Don't do it. Don't even think about it.

Why not?

First of all, because it's wrong. If you engage in unethical behavior, you're going to corrupt yourself. This may sound like a bunch of mumbo-jumbo, but it's true. If you cheat in school, three things can happen:

1. You will eventually feel guilty. Your skill at cheating will eat away at your heart, and you'll know the success you've attained has been tainted by the fact that you were dishonest. You may eventually find yourself surrounded by people who are successful in business and you'll know, in your heart, that you don't deserve to be there. The truly sad part is that you'll never be able to re-do your mistake. If you cheated in high school or college, those days are gone forever, and you'll be stuck with the bitter memory.

2. You'll get caught. Teachers are smart. They've read hundreds of term papers and they can spot the ones that are fake. They know you and your work, and will recognize a weird variation from what you've previously turned in. And you know, of course, that the guy who sold you a term paper has sold the same paper to a dozen other students, right? He's no dummy—he wants to maximize his profits. Your teacher will see your fake term paper and say to herself, "Well, here's another one I'm going to send to the principal. Too bad!"

3. You'll cheat yourself out of something you needed. The education system is far from perfect, but it is generally designed so that each step builds on the skills and knowledge of the step before it. Cheating *may* go unnoticed, and you *may* not feel guilt, but even in that best case scenario, you will be missing critical information when you come to the next grade or college class. And because you cheated, you don't know precisely what you don't know. Which often means that to pass, you have to cheat *more*. The cycle is exhausting. Cheat too much, and you'll likely get caught. In a worst-case scenario this can result in expulsion, with disastrous consequences for your academic record and college acceptance prospects. Even if you luck out and don't get caught you'll potentially be unable to get or hold a job because you'll find yourself competing against your peers, who did the work.

If you use AI to write a term paper, two things can happen:

1. You'll get a lousy term paper that looks like it was written by a machine, and your teacher may very well use AI to detect

machine-made or plagiarized papers. One of the most popular AI-powered plagiarism detectors is Turnitin, which—this is true—is designed to detect if a student's report has been created by an AI algorithm such as ChatGPT. This is possible because AI algorithms like Chat GPT are trained on millions of sample documents, and if you give it a command such as "Write a 5,000-word essay on Napoleon Bonaparte," it will churn out the same report each time, using the same references and composing its sentences in the same way. The patterns of language used by ChatGPT can be detected both by human readers and by algorithms including Turnitin.

You may think you're ahead of the pack by using AI to write your paper—but your teacher is probably one step ahead of you.

It's not worth it.

2. If you cheat on a test with a group of peers and one gets caught, do you think they're going to keep quiet about the part *you* played? That may happen in gangster movies, but in real life, to redeem themselves, or lessen their punishment, they will turn you in.

The bottom line is that your personal honor and integrity are priceless. It's yours and yours alone, and to sacrifice it for short-term gain is extremely foolish. You're literally better off if you go to your teacher and say, "I'm sorry, I didn't do the paper. What can I do to make up for it?"

TAKE ACTION!

- Think about your relationship with your school. Are you happy there, or not so much? If you're unhappy with the classes you must take, are there any subjects that truly excite you? Focus on those and ace them. Be a superstar. With subjects that you must take but don't like, just do your very best—you don't want them dragging down your GPA.

- It's always good if you can discuss your problems with your parents or guardians, but sometimes this is not possible. Do you have a counselor at school with whom you can talk honestly? State laws vary about how much your parents or guardians need to know about what you discuss. Just ask your counselor and he or she will give you the facts about confidentiality.

- How's your reading level? If you enjoy reading, learning becomes much easier and more fun. Keep reading!

- Do you have trouble reading? You may have a condition that's not your fault and is treatable. Talk to your parents or guardians, or to a teacher, and see if you can get tested by a professional.

- Are you ever tempted to cheat? If so, remember that school is designed to give you the tools you need to succeed in life and make a successful transition to independence and adulthood, and this includes developing high ethics. Stay honest and do the best you can every day.

4

Get a Job and Earn
While You Learn

The way to get started is to quit talking and begin doing.

— Walt Disney

As you journey from adolescence to adulthood, one of the most rewarding things you can do is get a job and make your own money.

Here's why.

When you perform a regular job outside the home, you'll receive three big benefits.

1. You'll get real-world work experience. You'll learn new skills, interact with a variety of people (including many adults), and have the opportunity to solve problems that matter.

2. You'll make your own money. There's no feeling quite like earning a paycheck with your name on it. It's an important step toward independence and thriving adulthood. Usually, your parents or guardians will insist you save some of it while giving yourself a small allowance to spend. You may also earn money towards your college expenses.

3. You'll build a feeling of personal satisfaction for having taken a step toward self-sufficiency as well as adding something of value to your community. When you're a little kid, the world can seem like a big mysterious place, and even scary. When you hold down a job—even for a few weeks over the summer—it can give you a boost of self-confidence and a feeling that you deserve a place in the adult world.

The Summer Job

For many young adults, the very first real job they get is during summer vacation. If you live in the suburbs, summer jobs could include being a lifeguard, golf caddy, babysitter, retail clerk, supermarket bagger, lawn care person, camp counselor, pool cleaner, theater usher, or many others. In cities, you can find work through a community, city, or state youth employment agency. You may find opportunities at restaurants, art museums, cultural centers, hospitals, private companies, recreation departments, the YMCA, and more.

Many high schools and most colleges have job centers that can help you find a summer job. Your parents or guardians may also know a business owner who has an opening.

The big question is this: "What job should I get?"

The answer is found within one of two options.

Here's **option #1**. If you have a strong area of interest and a career goal, then you should look for a job in your chosen field. If you're a computer person, look for a job in information technology. If you are interested in business, get an office job. If you like sports, try to find a job with a local team, sports venue, or sports broadcaster.

Sometimes a summer job can open the door to a lifelong career. When she was 18 years old, a student named Mary Barra took a summer job at a General Motors factory in Detroit, where she lived. This was in the year 1980, and she wanted to make money for her college education. She liked cars, and her job was to inspect fender panels and hoods on Pontiac Grand Prix vehicles.

She earned her degree in engineering and kept working at GM. She rose up through the ranks of the huge company, and after a succession of increasingly senior positions, on January 14, 2014, Mary Barra was named chief executive officer (CEO) of General Motors. She was the first woman to ever lead a major auto manufacturer. In January 2016 she cemented her success by becoming chairperson of the board, leading a global company with $156 billion in revenues and 167,000 employees.

You never know where a summer job might lead!

Here's **option #2**. If you have no idea of your career path and are open to new experiences, when looking for a summer job, find the weirdest one you can! Do something outside of your comfort zone. I know someone who, during the summer after his freshman year at college, got a job as an all-night donut maker in a donut shop. His shift started at eight o'clock in the evening and lasted until they had made all of the next day's donuts, which was four or five o'clock in the morning. He got home at dawn and slept all day. This was something he would never do as a career—but it was an unforgettable life experience. He was immersed in a way of life he otherwise would never have known, and saw the nocturnal life of the city. By seeing it first-hand, it became both less mysterious to him and more interesting. He also learned all about making donuts!

Unusual summer jobs include dog kennel worker, space camp counselor, birthday party clown, paintball referee, whale watch crew member, marina dockhand… The list is endless.

Many famous people have had interesting summer jobs. Comedian Jay Leno worked in the kitchen at a McDonald's franchise. "That was very impressive to me," Leno told author Cody Teets. "The standards for quality were quite high. It was one of those life lessons I never forgot."[40]

Entrepreneur and former CEO of Yahoo, Marissa Mayer, began her summer job career at age sixteen as a checkout clerk in the County Market in Wausau, Wisconsin. As she told *Fortune*, "I learned that speed mattered. They measured our items per minute rate during each shift, and the only way to be eligible to work an Express Lane was to do forty items per minute consistently over an eight-hour shift."[41]

Here's my story.

When I immigrated, I was an IT engineer holding a Cisco professional certificate. I wished I could have worked as a network admin, but I guess at that time I didn't know how to sell my resume. None of my job interviews resulted in a job offer.

While I was studying for my master's degree, I needed a job to pay my bills. So I got a job in telemarketing, selling alarm systems on the phone. I was making cold calls, and it was the toughest job I've ever had. It was definitely neither my specialty nor my dream job.

As a telemarketer, I learned many life lessons, one of which was to be unfailingly nice on the phone with the people I called, because *their* job was tough, too. I also found out how strong the survival instinct can be. It led me to places I never thought I could reach, helped me expand my resilience, and taught me delayed gratification.

Even though I hated this job, I had the highest sales performance. My colleagues often asked me, "How can you perform so well in a job you hate?"

The fact is, I was so scared to lose the only job I could find that I worked hard to keep it. I needed to survive, and losing it would derail my studies.

I found many character-building benefits from having a job in sales and customer service, which served me well later in my professional life. I learned to treat my colleagues and bosses in a customer service mode. That means when I interact with them, I show empathy and active listening to understand their needs and concerns, and to find solutions where everyone benefits. By taking this approach, I see that people value me and like working with me because they feel valued as well.

It also helped me succeed in job interviews by selling my unique profile, and ultimately to coach other people in my community to do the same. To this day, they call me to give them advice on job interviews.

I learned this the hard way, but today I thank God for giving me the chance to experience it. I believe everyone should try sales and customer service. When you think about it, in the workplace, everyone is a customer, including the people you work with. When you approach your job—any job—with a service mindset, by helping others succeed, your success will follow.

How to Get a Summer Job

Most summer jobs for young adults are *entry-level*. This means that the employer does not expect you to have a lengthy work history and you don't need a formal resume. Typically you apply by filling out an application, either in person or online. Just make sure you answer each question completely and truthfully. The application may ask you to list any previous jobs you've had, but if you're a high school or college student, your lack of job experience may not matter. If you need to fill out a physical application with a pen, be sure to write clearly. Don't forget to provide your contact information!

If you get called for an interview, be sure to follow the guidelines in chapter 2, "Self-Care." Have a clean and neat appearance. Don't smell, either of BO or heavy perfume. Leave the earbuds at home. Wear the clothes you wear to school, including shoes—no flip-flops. If your new employer has a dress code, he or she will tell you at the interview. Above all, look alert and interested. No employer wants to hire a slouching kid who won't make eye contact.

And *be on time.* No excuses!

Don't worry about your skills—your employer will teach you how to do the job. Be a fast learner and don't make the same mistake twice. No drugs, no drinking, no smoking!

You may end up loving your job, like Mary Barra, or use it for life experience, like Jay Leno. Either way is okay. Do a good job, have fun, and be a positive presence in the workplace.

W-2 and Tax Forms

In the United States, if you work for an employer for any length of time, at any age, and are paid more than $600 per year, you'll receive an Internal Revenue Service (IRS) Form W-2. They are produced by employers at the end of every year or, if you're a summer employee, you might get yours soon after you leave the job.

The W-2 form shows important information about the money paid to you by your employer, the amount of taxes withheld from your paycheck, benefits provided, and other financial information for the year. You use this form when filing your federal and state taxes.

You'll notice the phrase "taxes withheld." Here's what it means.

Adults who earn a certain minimum amount of money must file a tax return every year with the federal Internal Revenue Service. They may or may not owe taxes, but they need to file. Some states also require earners to file state income tax forms. To make paying taxes less painful, from each paycheck the IRS will take or "withhold" a portion of your expected annual tax. It will also take Social Security taxes.

At the end of the year, if too much has been withheld, the IRS sends you a refund. If for some reason you owe the IRS money, you need to pay it. But many workers get refunds, which seems like "free money" because it was surrendered imperceptibly during the year.

As for filing taxes, many young people can claim to be dependents of their parents up to a certain age. But if you're old enough and earn enough to file a tax return, you must report all employment income, regardless of when you earn it, including income reported on a W-2 form by your summer employer. If in doubt, ask your parents or guardians, or find a local tax professional. There are also many charitable tax preparation services for low-income people.

If you work as an *independent contractor* and not an employee, and you earn more than $600 in a year, your employer must send you an IRS Form 1099-NES. It stands for "non-employee compensation." The employer must also send a copy to the IRS, so the agency may expect you to report it and pay any required tax. Consult your parents, guardians, or a tax professional.

When you're first hired, your employer may ask you to fill out an IRS Form W-4, Employee's Withholding Allowance Certificate. Employers use this form to calculate how much federal income tax to withhold from your pay. If you're an independent contractor—like a babysitter or gig worker—your employer may ask you for an IRS Form W-9, which is similar to a W-4.

If any of these forms confuse you, ask your employer! Just remember that your employer may ask you to fill out a tax form, and this is perfectly normal.

Neurodiversity in the Workplace

In the old days, people talked a lot about what was "normal" human behavior. In books, movies, and popular culture, you'd see examples and discussions about what "normal" people did as opposed to "other people" or "deviant people." The suggestion was that you couldn't be a good, moral, productive citizen unless you looked or thought a certain way.

Fortunately, in the United States and many other industrialized nations, our understanding of people, and in particular the wonders of the human brain, is expanding and getting deeper. We now know that individuals can reach a goal or complete a task by approaching it in different ways. This flexibility is made possible because the human brain has many different ways of functioning and solving problems. This new insight has led to a re-defining of what we call "normal" to include people who were once mistakenly marginalized or excluded, but who in fact can be as productive as anyone else.

The name for this new understanding is "neurodiversity." The term was coined in 1997 by Australian sociologist Judy Singer, who herself is autistic.

What does this word mean?

You've probably heard the word "diversity" used in reference to everyday society, such as at work or at school. It means the practice or quality of including or involving people from a range of different genders, sexual orientations, social and ethnic backgrounds, and even ages. Diversity in an organization or workplace is regarded as a strength and asset. Why? Because the best decisions and best outcomes are achieved when many viewpoints are represented. Different people perceive problems in different ways, and the most effective solution is one that combines the varied perspectives, opinions, and experiences of all individuals involved. The word "neuro" simply means "brain" or "thinking." It's the basis for the word "neurodivergent," which means having a brain that works differently from the average or "neurotypical" person.

The neurodivergent person may show differences in social preferences or ways of learning, perceiving the environment, or communicating. Rather than assuming there is something defective when a person's brain doesn't operate similarly to others, and that "normal = good" and "abnormal = bad," neurodiversity recognizes that the many ways the human brain operates lie along a broad spectrum. There is no "normal" or "abnormal" anymore because "different" means "neurodivergent." Many people use neurodiversity as a general term used to describe various ways the brain processes information, including dyslexia, dyspraxia (a neurologically based physical disorder), social anxiety disorders, autism/Asperger syndrome, and attention-deficit/hyperactivity disorder (ADHD). In fact, when talking about autism, we use the term "autism spectrum disorder" (ASD), which refers to a broad range of conditions influenced by a combination of environmental and genetic factors, giving each person with autism a distinct set of strengths and challenges.

When an employer hires a neurodiverse person, they focus on three key questions. The first two are what he or she would ask any candidate, while the third is for the neurodivergent individual:

1. Is this person productive? Can they do the job?

2. Is this person capable of working with others harmoniously?

3. Can any special needs of this person be accommodated by the workplace?

Because many neurodiverse people have challenges conducting interviews in the traditional neurotypical manner, in the old days, neurodiverse candidates who would have scored a solid "yes" to all three questions were rejected early in the hiring process. But interviewing skills are not necessarily the same as job skills, and progressive companies are learning that many neurodiverse employees are in fact superstars in their area of specialization. *Harvard Business Review* noted that at Hewlett Packard Enterprise (HPE), their neurodiverse software testers observed that before a software launch, one client's projects always seemed to go into crisis mode. These testers, who were personally intolerant of any form of chaos, objected to HPE's acceptance of a certain level of disorder in the development process. This led the company to successfully redesign the launch process, save money, and better serve its clients.[42]

It's worth noting that while many neurodivergent people do not see themselves as "disabled," the Americans with Disabilities Act of 1990 (ADA) covers neurodiverse individuals, which means that they have a right to "reasonable accommodations," not only to do their job, but also to the interview process to get that job, and to "enjoy equal benefits and privileges of employment." The best way for a company to comply with ADA requirements is to simply create a company culture that values *everyone's* individuality equally. For example, Google has done this; they have a special test to detect neurodivergent candidates because their sense of detail and rigor are very valuable in the tech industry.

When you join a company, you might have the opportunity to work on a team with neurodiverse people. Don't worry! Get ready for a fascinating experience! Every individual, whether neurotypical or neurodivergent, brings their unique strengths, making each interaction different and enriching for everyone involved. Embracing this diversity not only fosters a more inclusive work environment but opens doors to personal growth and a sense of fulfillment for all team members.

Here are a few things you'll want to keep in mind:

- Be aware of your own unconscious biases and expectations of others. Keep an open mind about what other people need to be successful.
- Focus on the strengths of each individual. Some neurodivergent workers have exceptional capabilities, and that's why they were hired!
- Recognize your colleagues' unique needs and preferences. Some may prefer a very quiet environment, while others may be sensitive to quick movements, smells, or colors.
- Speak plainly. Many neurodivergent people are literal and do not understand things like sarcasm and insinuations.Follow the individual's lead in what makes them comfortable.
- Relax, be happy, be a good teammate—and you may even make a new friend!

My 7 Tips for How to Excel at Your Job!

Here are my top 7 tips for succeeding at your job:

1. Learn through observation what is acceptable and professional behavior, and follow suit.

2. To speed up the learning curve, listen more than you talk.

3. Practice humility. To be coachable, listen to the coach and learn. Take notes to avoid making the coach repeat the same thing more than once.

4. When you don't know, say, "I don't know." But meanwhile, try to find out on your own. Do your research, ask a more experienced and trusted colleague, ask for specific training if available, or simply ask your boss if they can help you find the information.

5. Be in solution mode, not in problem mode. Anyone can point out a problem. You stand out when you can provide the solution! As the old saying goes, "Winners find solutions, while losers find excuses!"

6. Give it your best and allow yourself to make mistakes. Everybody makes mistakes, even your boss! Acknowledge the mistake, fix it, learn from it, and move on.

7. Never talk about anyone behind their back. Sooner or later, they'll find out. Be the person who can always be trusted.

Become an Entrepreneur

In this chapter, we've talked about working by getting hired by an employer who has an established business.

But that's not the only way to earn money, gain work experience, and maybe even launch a career. Instead of hoping to get hired by a business owner, the alternative is to start your own business for yourself. That means becoming an entrepreneur.

With your own business, you choose what you want to do to earn money—either provide a service or sell a product. You find the customers, you do the work (or hire someone to help you), and you collect the money. Generally, the harder you work, the more money you're going to make.

Here's an example of an entrepreneur who built an amazing career.

In 1989, Brian Scudamore was a 19-year-old high school dropout in Vancouver, Canada. He had dreams of going to college, but he had no money for tuition. One day, while waiting in the drive-through lane of a McDonald's restaurant, Scudamore happened to see an old, beat-up pickup truck emblazoned with the words, "Mark's Hauling." The truck was for a trash removal company.

"I can do that!" Scudamore thought.

For $700 Scudamore bought an old Ford F-100 pickup truck and then spent another $300 on fliers and business cards. This $1,000 was his entire life savings. Even though the business was just himself, he called it the Rubbish Boys.

"I wanted it to sound bigger," he told *CNBC Make It*.[43]

In a few weeks, Scudamore had made back his investment. After a year, he had made a profit of about $1,700, which he used to pay for his college tuition.

After many ups and downs, by 1997, the Rubbish Boys business had reached $1 million in annual revenue. Scudamore aggressively expanded his company by selling franchises to other people who wanted to get into the business.

Today the company, which in 1999 was renamed 1-800-GOT-JUNK?, operates junk-removal franchises in roughly 160 locations in the U.S., Canada, and Australia. Valued at over $300 million, it's the center of a bigger family of brands launched by Scudamore that includes a house-painting company, WOW 1 Day Painting, and a home-detailing business, Shack Shine, which Scudamore founded in 2010 and 2015, respectively.

"Did I know that day that this would be something much bigger than just a way to pay for college? No," Scudamore said. "But I knew that if I picked something and I committed and stuck with it, the passion for building a business would soon follow."

The interesting thing about how Brian Scudamore became an entrepreneur is that it wasn't the result of a grand scheme or detailed business plan. He literally saw a junk removal truck and a light bulb went off in his head. He had an idea and he pursued it; and when faced with challenges he persevered. He said, "I can do this," and he never gave up.

A business can be just about anything. The classic example of an entrepreneur is the kid who operates a lemonade stand on the side of the road. Since you're older, you could offer a dog-walking service, be a nanny, make products like soap or scarves, operate a car wash, mow lawns, build websites, make YouTube videos, be a tutor to little kids—the ideas are limitless.

To learn about how to start a business, start online. Go to your favorite search engine and simply type in "How to start a business."

You'll find loads of information on how to do it, from government agencies to magazines to business "incubators" that offer free or low-cost advice. If you need legal advice, look for a clinic offering services for cheap rates. You can also enroll in a course at your local community college, or even just buy a book!

The thing is to follow Walt Disney's advice—don't talk about it, do it!

Gig Work

We've talked about traditional jobs and entrepreneurship, but there's one sector of work that combines the two: gig work. Sites like Upwork and Fiverr allow you to sell marketable skills from the comfort of your own home. Taskrabbit allows you to make money doing odd jobs without the hassle of setting up advertising and managing a website. If you can legally drive, Uber, Lyft, Doordash, Instacart, and other rideshare or delivery services offer opportunities to use your car as a way to make money. In fact, Doordash and other meal delivery services will sometimes offer the option to deliver by bicycle, eliminating the need to buy an expensive car to do the job! This is popular in big cities.

Gig work offers the opportunity to set your own hours, which can be a particularly attractive option for students. You can work as much or as little as you like, and can sign up for more than one site, allowing you to work a different job every day. While the money is not always the best, you are not at the mercy of an employer. So, if you find yourself strapped for cash, you *can* just work more hours.

Sounds great, right? Well, there are some downsides to it.

First, you're what's called an "independent contractor." That means you have zero benefits. You can't get insurance through your job, you have no paid time off, you don't get overtime or holiday pay, and *most importantly* you are responsible for withholding your own taxes. At the end of the year, instead of a W2 and a tax refund, you get a 1099 (an independent contractor tax form) and a tax *bill*. That means that instead of the IRS owing you money at the end of the year, you owe *them*. So be cautious: many sites involve fees or hourly rate deductions for using their platform, and Uber, at the time of writing, does not refund you for gas or vehicle repairs. These are your "operating expenses." It's possible to claim these back in your taxes as business mileage, but meticulous record-keeping is needed. If you're going to do gig work, it can be worth the time and money to talk to a tax professional about the best way to manage your taxes.

The second downside is discipline. A regular job has a schedule for you to adhere to, a boss that directs and determines what you do each day, and if you miss a shift or show up late, there are consequences. The only person that's responsible for, and dependent on, you showing up for gig work is you. You can take off all the days you want, but if you're not careful, you'll find yourself without any money! If you decide to do gig work, you may want to take a week to a month to try it (and remember to withhold taxes!) Figure out how much you make per hour, or per day. Then calculate how many hours or days a week you need to work in order to pay your bills. You may be surprised to find that you can take more days off than a traditional job, or realize that gig work simply can't support you. But once you have those hard numbers, it's up to you to put the work in and show up day in and day out to make the money you need.

The third and final downside to gig work is that, at the end of the day, you're marketing yourself while representing a company. Just like being an entrepreneur, it's your responsibility to engage with every customer and provide them with the most positive experience possible. However, pure entrepreneurship means being accountable to nobody; you're the boss, and you can pick and choose your clients, while in the gig economy, you're a contractor, which means you have rules to follow and your job security relies on your ability to consistently deliver 5-star service. So, you need to avoid customers filing complaints with your parent company about your performance. Since you're likely to interact with dozens of essentially random customers each day, upset someone or deliver late, and with the tap of a finger, you get a dreaded 1-star review from a disgruntled customer, which can damage your reputation and credibility. Potential customers rely on reviews to make decisions about whom to hire, and a series of negative reviews can result in a decrease in job opportunities and income. So, every customer interaction is an opportunity to shine or fall short.

This blending of entrepreneurship and a traditional job can either be your best asset if you're a people person with great attention to detail, or your worst enemy if you struggle to connect with people. Take the time to think through your options. For some people, gig work is a fun, exciting experience. For others, it's a necessary evil. Be careful to figure out which it is for you before you commit to it as your only source of income.

TAKE ACTION!

- Before school gets out for the summer, start looking around for a summer job. You don't want to be shut out of the best opportunities!

- Do you have an existing area of interest? Look for a job in that industry, or make your own business by being an entrepreneur. Are you undecided? Try a job that's unusual or out of your comfort zone.

- Try to find a job that involves either learning a skill that you don't currently have or working with the public in customer service. Then at the end of the summer, you'll have valuable experience that will serve you for life.

- For entry-level jobs, you'll fill out an application and go for an interview. Be clean, neat, alert, and on time!

- Your employer may ask you to fill out a tax form. This is normal. If you have questions, take the form home and ask your parents or guardians for advice.

- Reflect on your personality, skills, and resources in considering gig work. But remember: you will receive zero benefits and will have the added burden of withholding your own taxes. Gig work offers freedom, but can you hold yourself accountable to deliver 5-star service and transform a flexible schedule into sustainable income?

- Save your money! Agree to spend a small portion on yourself, but save the rest for college.

5

Be the Boss of Your Cash

Beware of little expenses; a small leak will sink a great ship.
— Benjamin Franklin

We began the previous chapter by reminding you—perhaps needlessly—that one of the greatest pleasures of adult life is the ability to work and earn your own money, to do with as you please.

In this chapter, we're going to begin by reminding you of the opposite: that few things in life will make you more miserable more quickly than frittering away your hard-earned money on a bunch of stuff you don't need and barely want. The result could involve returning to your previous living situation, if this option is still available.

Finances can be a challenging tug-of-war. On one hand, it's a great feeling to have a credit card in your pocket or Apple Pay on your phone, allowing you to get whatever you want in a single swipe—anything from a gourmet dinner at your favorite restaurant to a new phone, pair of shoes, concert tickets, or an outfit for that special event. But all those little—and big—things that you buy can quickly add up, and before you know it, your bank account balance is down to zero and you still have another week to go before payday—not to mention your rent being due.

One thing you should never, *ever* do is get a payday loan to cover such shortfalls. *Never, ever.* But more about that later.

The goal of this chapter is to arm you with the information you need to avoid falling into a fiscal hole, and to build up a savings cushion for special occasions, your education, or maybe even buying a house someday.

Let's begin by reviewing some basic concepts that you need to understand so that you can effectively manage the money you earn.

Money Management 101

Let's say you have a job or a small business, like lawn mowing or babysitting. You're making some money. It feels good, doesn't it? When you were a little kid, you could keep your pennies and dollars in a piggy bank. Life was simple! But now life is more complicated, the amounts of money are larger, and you need a way to manage your funds.

You need to open a bank account.

A bank is a financial institution that is licensed by a state and regulated by the U.S. government, which can accept and hold checking and savings deposits, make loans, and issue credit cards. Banks also provide additional services such as selling certificates of deposit (CDs), offering individual retirement accounts (IRAs), and providing currency exchange and safe deposit boxes.

You need to open a bank account for two reasons.

1. If you have a job and your employer pays you with a paycheck (usually every week or two weeks), you need a secure and recognized place to deposit your paycheck and turn it into cash. Your paycheck may be given or mailed to you as a paper document (an actual check) that you deposit, or your employer may offer direct deposit, in which your pay is electronically deposited directly into your bank account. The vast majority of

workers choose direct deposit because it's faster, more convenient, and saves paper.

2. You need a place to store your money that is safe and provides a platform from which you can pay your bills and write checks. One of the great benefits of a bank account is that most banks offer fraud protection, which means that if someone hacks into your account and tries to steal your money, the bank will take responsibility. In addition, through the Federal Deposit Insurance Corporation (FDIC), the federal government guarantees deposits of up to $250,000 per depositor per bank, which protects you in case the bank itself goes out of business.

The least optimal thing you can do with your paycheck is to take it to a check-cashing service, which is usually a storefront in a neighborhood. They will cash your check but they will take a hefty fee, which varies by state; typically it will range from 1 percent as high as 12 percent of the value of your check. For a $1,000 check, you'll be paying from $10 to $120 to *get your own money*.

Crazy, right? That's why you need a bank account.

Yes, banks do charge fees. They need to earn a profit, and fees are a big part of that. Many banks have been accused of charging too many fees. They could include:

- Monthly maintenance fee, just for having a checking account.
- Overdraft fee, for taking out more than you have in your account.
- Check fees for writing checks.
- Out-of-network ATM fee, for using another bank's ATM.
- Inactivity fee. Yes, some banks charge you for doing nothing!

How can you protect yourself from excessive fees? Read the fine print of your account agreement and learn the various fees that the bank could charge you. Overall, the best way to avoid fees is to keep a sufficient amount of money in your account. This needs to be whatever your bank requires as a minimum balance to avoid many fees. Generally, the more money you have in your checking account, the fewer fees the bank will try to charge you.

Never write a check and say, "I'll cover it before it hits my bank account." Only spend what you actually have in your account.

Opening a Bank Account

To open a bank account, you simply apply in person or online. After 9/11, the U.S. government tightened the rules on customer identification (also called Know Your Customer rules), and everyone who opens a bank account needs to prove their identity to the bank.

For any type of bank account, you're likely to need the following:

1. A valid, government-issued photo ID. This could be a driver's license or a passport. If you don't drive, you should be able to get a state ID card at your local Department of Motor Vehicles office.

2. Personal information including your address, birthdate, Social Security number or taxpayer identification number, or phone number.

3. Most banks require an initial deposit amount. This makes sense—why would you open an account with no money?

4. If you are not yet 18, you'll need a co-signer. Ask a parent or legal guardian to sign the papers with the bank.

If you're undocumented (and don't have a Social Security number, for example), you may be able to open an account with a variety of other documents that prove who you are. An officer at your chosen bank will be able to provide guidance.

Checking or Savings Account?

Often, an account you open at a bank will include both a checking and savings account linked together, but sometimes you only get one. Here are the benefits of both types and their differences.

Checking accounts are primarily for accessing your money for daily use. You can write a paper check to pay a bill, use your debit card, or even make an electronic transfer using your bank's internal system or a third-party platform such as PayPal, Venmo, or Apple Pay.

Most banks have phone apps that allow you to see your account activity, transfer funds, and even deposit paper checks using your phone's camera.

Because a checking account requires the bank to provide more services, there are always more fees associated with a checking account.

Savings accounts are typically used to save money for a financial goal or specific purpose. You're supposed to deposit your money in a savings account and leave it there undisturbed. The bank will impose limits on how often you can make withdrawals. Savings accounts are interest bearing, which means the bank pays you a small amount every month for having your money there.

With your bank account information accessible through your phone app or through the internet on your desktop computer, there's *no reason* to not know how much money you have in your checking account! If you use your debit card to pay for something, your payment will usually appear within minutes on your account transactions screen, and your account balance will be updated. If you make a deposit, it will also show up quickly, but keep in mind that while your deposit may have been *received* by your bank, it takes time—sometimes up to a full day—for the bank to process your deposit and make the funds available to you.

Check your bank balances regularly. Some people do it every day. If you see a transaction that you don't recognize, and you think something's wrong, call your bank or visit a branch office as soon as possible.

The Good and Bad of Credit Cards

The subject of borrowing money is a touchy one, especially for things that (in theory at least) you could save up to buy.

Many people think you should never borrow money. This idea was summed up by Shakespeare in his play *Hamlet*, in which Polonius advises his son, Laertes, "Neither a borrower, nor a lender be. For loan oft loses both itself and friend. And borrowing dulls the edge of husbandry." In simple terms, if you lend money to a friend, you'll probably lose both the money and the friend. If you borrow too much or too often, keeping track of what you owe and who you owe it to can make your finances a nightmare. On the other hand, many big purchases in life, such as buying a house or a car, are difficult to make without borrowing the money to do so.

Borrowing should be done very carefully. The most common way that people borrow money on a day-to-day basis is by using credit cards. And sadly, one of the main causes of financial misery for young people—for anyone, in fact—is the misuse of credit cards.

The concept of a credit card, like Visa or Mastercard, is that the issuer of the card is willing to extend to you a *short-term unsecured loan.* When you use a Visa card to buy a new computer, you're not using your own money. You're *borrowing* the money from your Visa card issuer, usually a bank. The Visa company needs to make a profit, so they'll charge you interest on any amount you haven't paid back. Interest rates fluctuate; historically, they've been around 10 to 20 percent, but they can be higher. The longer you take to pay back what you've borrowed, the more interest you're going to pay. If you fail to pay on time, your "balance due" will literally explode because the interest charges will keep *compounding*—that is to say, the interest you owe on your unpaid balance will keep increasing. For example, if you spend $500 on your Visa card, then your first month's interest might make the total you owe $500 plus $50 in interest, or $550.

If you don't pay the $550, then the next month you might owe $605.

And if you still don't pay, the next month you'll owe $665.50.

And so on! This is because with compound interest, the new interest charges are calculated based on the total you owe. In the above example, in the first month you'll owe $500 plus 10% interest = $550.

In the second month you'll owe $550 plus 10% interest = $605.

In the third month, you'll owe $605 plus 10% interest = $655.50.

So if you bought a coat for $500 and didn't pay your Visa bill for three months, that coat will have actually cost you $655.50, plus any late fees the credit card company can hit you with. (Yes, they can do that too.)

So be very careful, and *never* use your credit card to buy something unless you can pay it back when your payment is due. If you don't pay your credit card bill by the due date, you'll get hit with late fees and rising interest payments.

One more thing—if you have an American Express card, it might work a little differently. Some Amex cards are what people used to call "charge cards" because according to your contract, you *must* pay your balance *in full* at the end of each month. You cannot carry over a balance from month to month like a credit card. Amex cards have traditionally been known for having generous "rewards" in the form of points that you can use to buy stuff, and the Amex charge cards generally have the best rewards. As with any credit card, if you get an Amex card, be sure to read the contract very carefully and know your responsibilities.

If used properly, credit cards, and credit in general, can be very useful to you. Access to credit can allow you to make purchases and pay them off over time, as opposed to saving your money little by little to buy the same item much later in your life. If you had to literally save $400,000 to buy a house and pay cash for it, by the time you could make the purchase you'd be too old to start a family! Taking out a mortgage allows you to buy the house while you're still young.

Your ability to get any type of loan, including a credit card, depends upon your *credit rating*. Your credit rating is a reflection of how lenders perceive you as a *risk*. You want them to see you as being *low risk*—that is, you want them to say, "We should lend to this person because we are certain he or she will pay us back." If you are perceived as being high risk, lenders will be unwilling to lend you money.

Your level of risk is indicated by your *credit score*. This is a number assigned to you by a credit rating company called FICO and used by the three big credit rating services—TransUnion, Experian, and Equifax. (These services also use a rating system called VantageScore, but the basics are the same.) Your FICO score will range between 300 and 850. The higher your score, the more credit you can get. From 300 to 629 is bad. A good score is anything above 690.

Your FICO score is based on several factors. The first two are the most important:

1. Your payment history, which is whether you pay your bills on time. Paying on time will raise your credit score.

2. Credit utilization, which is how much of your available credit you are using. Having more available credit but using less of it will raise your credit score.

3. How long you've had credit. The longer, the better.

4. Your mix of credit types. These include credit cards, store credit cards, car loans, bank loans, and mortgage loans. The bigger the mix, the better.

5. How frequently and recently you've applied for credit. Applying for credit too often (in their eyes) will lower your credit score.

You are entitled to see your full credit report anytime from an online service like Credit Karma. It's a free service and will not affect your credit score. Credit Karma will also send you an email alert when your credit score changes for any reason.

The good part about credit cards is that they represent a pool of funds that you can access in an emergency. It's like having a financial safety net. In fact, the best way to use credit cards is to have one or two and *never use them*. One trick is to keep them frozen in a block of ice in the freezer, so it takes real effort to get to them.

Why would you do this? Because when you're granted a credit card, it comes with a maximum credit limit—say, $10,000. That "available credit" is the amount you're able to borrow. It's reported to the three big credit rating services—TransUnion, Experian, and Equifax. This is the important part: The fact that you have access to $10,000 in credit *and don't use it* will boost your credit rating. Lenders like to see that you *could* borrow money but *don't*. That makes you a better credit risk. On the other hand, if you have one credit card with a credit limit of $10,000 and you've "maxed out" your card and you owe the full $10,000, that's *bad*. It tells the credit agencies that you may be in over your head and cannot pay your bills.

This is what the credit companies mean by "credit utilization." Lenders like to see that you *could* borrow lots of money ("utilize your credit") but you *don't*.

It takes financial discipline to own one or more credit cards and never use them, or use them and pay them back immediately. Even if you really want something, you need to be able to say "no" to yourself.

Earlier we mentioned that a credit card is an "unsecured" loan. This means that you don't need to provide collateral to "secure" it. If you fail to pay your credit card bill, Visa cannot come after you and seize your property. But Visa *will* give you a horrible credit score, and ensure that no one else will extend credit to you until you take steps to repair your credit score. You don't want this! Don't burn your credit card company. You want to maintain a good credit score so that you can get a loan when you need to.

So, how do you get your first credit card?

Many young people who are under 18 and have no credit history begin by becoming an *authorized user* of their parent's or guardian's credit card. While the primary cardholder is responsible for paying the credit card bill, the young person can use the card and—this is the best part— become established as a user of credit with their own credit score.

If you're over 18, you can apply for various student credit cards. These cards generally have higher interest rates and lower spending limits than regular cards, but if you use them properly they should not be much more expensive than a regular card. You can also get a retail store credit card, which also may carry a higher interest rate as well as restrictions about where you can use it. But like a student credit card, if you use it properly and keep your balance low, they will help you build your credit score. Popular examples include the Prime Visa from Amazon, the Costco Anywhere Visa Card by Citi, and the Capital One Walmart Reward Mastercard.

If you have a low credit score (say, 500) and you cannot get a normal Visa, Mastercard, or Discover card because of your bad credit, to build up your good credit you can get a secured Visa where you *pay up front* a certain amount of money, like $200. Then as you use the card, you draw down your own money, and then pay it back like a regular credit card. You cannot draw more than is in your account. This may seem silly because you're spending your own money, but the good news is that secured Visa cards report to FICO, just like real cards do. So if you own a secured Visa card for a year, and keep it current, you'll see your credit score rise! Once your score rises high enough, you'll qualify for a real Visa card. Keep the original secured card as a backup, because the longer you keep it, the higher your credit score will go.

Other types of loans, particularly car loans and home mortgages, are secured by the car or home. If you fail to pay your car loan, the repossession company (the "repo man") will come and take your car. You can watch crazy YouTube videos about how tough these guys are. You don't want to mess with them!

Debit Cards vs. Credit Cards

On many retail checkout machines, the screen will ask you, "Credit or Debit?" This can be confusing, especially because it's the same card! Which should you choose?

When your card—usually a Visa or Mastercard—is used as a debit card (also known as online debit or PIN-based debit), the transaction is linked directly to your bank account. The moment you use a debit card, the money is instantly taken from your checking account. It's just like paying with cash.

With your debit card, you may be able to withdraw cash from your account. As you see during the checkout process, there might be a screen that asks, "Cash back?" with pre-set amounts indicated—$20, $40, and so forth. If you choose the cash back option, you'll have to enter your PIN. Otherwise, you may only have to hit the "approved" button. With small purchases, such as those under $25, you may not need to enter your PIN or sign when making a purchase, regardless of whether you choose debit or credit.

With the "credit" option (also known as offline debit or signature-based debit), you swipe or insert your card and then sign the screen to complete the purchase. Sometimes no signing is required.

Many retailers also offer "contactless payment," which means you simply bring your card to the checkout device and the sale is made. Such cards use radio frequency identification (RFID) technology and near-field communication (NFC) to process transactions in establishments that are equipped to do so. Contactless cards feature a Wi-Fi symbol on the front of the card. To use a contactless card, simply look for the same Wi-Fi symbol on the payment terminal. Tap your credit card on the symbol. After getting a payment confirmation, you're on your way!

In addition, some retailers including Whole Foods are experimenting with "Just Walk Out" technology that allows you to fill your shopping basket and "just walk out" of the store, and your card is automatically charged. This "frictionless" system is designed to save you time waiting in line at the checkout counter.

All of these technologies, designed to make it super-easy to pay, can also make it super-easy to *spend money you don't have*. If you use contactless payment systems, that's even more reason to frequently log into your bank account and review your transaction history for accuracy.

The trend is toward faster payment processing no matter how you use your bank card. While there is a difference in how your payment is processed by the card issuer, as previously mentioned, if you use your *bank debit card*, the money will come out of your checking account. But if you use a *real credit card*, then your bank or credit card company will *loan you the money* for your purchase, and you must be sure to pay it as soon as you receive the bill from your credit card company.

When you make a significant purchase with a card or app, you should know that generally the major credit cards (Visa, Mastercard, Discover, and American Express) have fraud protection policies, and you can dispute a charge that you think is erroneous or fraudulent. They also offer features including bonus points and easy access to services like travel insurance. But debit cards and many cash transfer apps have no such services or protection: Once you send your money, it's gone. If you have a dispute, you must deal directly with the person or business to whom you sent your cash.

To recap: Credit cards are good ways to build your credit rating, but you *must* keep your payments current! Most credit cards offer fraud protection. Debit cards and cash transfer apps are convenient, but may offer no protection from fraud or a simple mistake, and they do nothing to build your credit rating.

All major banks offer full online services. You can log on anytime from your phone or desktop and see your transactions and balances, often up to the minute. Make this a habit! Regularly check your accounts to see the activity and look for anything suspicious.

Funds Transfer Apps

There are many ways to transfer funds and make payments using your phone. In fact, you may go weeks or even months without ever handling physical cash!

Venmo offers a quick and easy way to spend, send, or transfer money to your bank account. Using the ACH network (a payment system that reaches all U.S. bank and credit union accounts), a standard bank transfer from your Venmo account to your bank checking account typically takes one to three business days to arrive. For a fee, you can also choose an instant transfer to a bank account or debit card, which arrives within 30 minutes. Venmo also offers a debit card that will allow you to make purchases directly from your balance. Venmo works with most U.S.-based banks.

Please be aware that Venmo was initially designed as an app for college kids to easily transfer small amounts of cash back and forth between themselves. You could "friend" someone, just like on Facebook, and view all your other friends. You could also see all the cash transfers between them! This might be fun on campus, but in the adult world it's not what you want. For this reason, most adults *do not* "friend" people with whom they exchange funds on Venmo. Keep your business private!

PayPal offers speed and convenience as well as PayPal's brand name awareness across the United States. It's easy to install and use, and fast and secure. It can hold money, like a bank, but your cash is not FDIC insured. Transaction fees are considered high. PayPal, like Venmo, offers a debit card that is linked directly to your balance.

WorldRemit has the flexibility to send funds to recipients in over 130 countries within minutes. Most transfers complete within 24 hours wherever recipients live in the world. It gives you various ways to send money—through cash pickup, bank transfer, mobile money, home delivery, and airtime top-up.

Cash App allows users to send funds via mobile app for free. It's very easy to use, and offers investment options, buying and selling bitcoin and getting special savings with "cash boosts." Like many money transfer apps, CashApp offers a debit card, and both free transfers to a linked bank account within 1-3 days, or an instant transfer to a linked debit card for a small fee.

Facebook Pay features easy transferring of small amounts of money through a familiar platform. You can use the app to make seamless and secure payments in select countries through WhatsApp, Portal, Meta Messenger, and Instagram.

Zelle is the choice for bank-to-bank transfers. You can go to your bank's website or to the mobile app to register with just an email address or phone number. Because it's bank-to-bank, your money is federally insured. It only works with U.S. banks, not foreign banks.

Apple Pay is built into every iPhone, Apple Watch, Mac, and iPad. If you have one of those devices, there's no separate app to download. It stores in Apple Wallet the cash you receive or want to send, and according to the company, Apple Pay is accepted at over 85 percent of retailers in the United States.

These are just a few! Choose the one(s) that work best for you, but be mindful of fees, and be sure to track your balances. Keep the bulk of your funds in an FDIC insured bank account, and only use these apps for everyday expenses.

Budgeting

You've probably heard your parents or guardians say, "You've got to live within your budget!"

This simply means one thing: *You have to earn more money than you spend.*

To put it another way: *Your expenses cannot exceed your income.*

Let's look at those two words—income and expenses.

Income

Your income is the amount of money that comes into your possession during a specific period of time—a week, a month, or a year.

There are two types of income.

Earned income is money that you make from working. For example, let's say you have a job that pays you $600 per week. Therefore, your monthly income will average $600 x 4 weeks = $2,400. Your annual income with paid vacation will be $600 x 52 weeks = $31,200.

Excluding any other sources of income, this is what you have to live on for the week, the month, and the year.

Generally, you receive your earned income while you're actually working. If you stop working—such as if you quit your job or get laid off—then your earned income will stop.

Unearned income, or passive income, is money that is paid to you because you own something of value that other people must pay to use, or money you receive when something of value that you own increases in value and you then sell it.

There are many categories of unearned income based on property ownership, and they include *rent,* received from people who use a building or house that you own; *interest,* which you receive from people to whom you have loaned money; and *profit,* received from your ownership of a business.

When you have a bank account and the bank pays you *interest* on your deposited money, that's a form of unearned income. When you buy shares of stock, and you hold them, the company may occasionally pay you a *dividend,* which is a small amount of money representing a portion of the profits of the company. If your shares of stock increase in value and you then sell them, the profit you receive is called *capital gains.*

Throughout your life, you may receive unearned income from a wide variety of other sources, such as:

- Inheritances.
- Gifts.
- Social Security benefits.
- Welfare benefits.
- Retirement accounts including 401(k)s, pensions, and annuities.
- Alimony.
- Veterans Affairs (VA) benefits.

Unearned income can be a source of incredible wealth; for example, it's estimated that Jeff Bezos's personal worth increases by $26 million *per day* based on the value of the Amazon.com stock that he owns. Unearned income can also take the form of royalties from works of art, books, or songs that you've created. The country singer Dolly Parton has been very smart about owning her own songs, and she receives millions of dollars in royalties from them every year. At age 20, Dolly started her own publishing company, and she owns her entire catalog of music, which consists of more than 3,000 song credits and is estimated to be worth at least $150 million. In 2021, Forbes reported that just two of her songs, "9 to 5" and "Jolene," earn about $6 million to $8 million in royalties per year. Every time one of her songs is played on the radio, purchased as a download, or used in a film, Dolly Parton receives a publishing fee.[44]

And by the way, Dolly Parton is well known for her charitable giving, and it's estimated that she donates over $1 million per year to philanthropic causes. Reading is a particular area of interest for her, and her Imagination Library is a non-profit charity dedicated to inspiring a love of reading by gifting books free of charge to children from birth to age five in the United States, Canada, United Kingdom, Australia, and Republic of Ireland.

While the idea of enjoying substantial unearned or passive income is a good goal to aim for, let's focus on the income you presently earn from your job (or jobs, if you have more than one).

The flip side of income is expenses.

Expenses

Your total expenses—meaning *every penny you spend for any purpose*—must not exceed your income during the same period.

There are many sneaky expenses that you may not think about. These include *taxes* of all types, *interest* on your credit card, and *fees*, such as bank fees. You'd be shocked to find out how quickly they can pile up!

Ideally, your income will always exceed your expenses, which will allow you to take the excess income and either save it or invest it. If you look at your bank account balance at any time, it must always be a positive number.

Here's something interesting to remember about the ratio of income to expenses. Imagine Sally makes $200,000 a year at her job and her expenses are $210,000 per year. It may seem at first glance that Sally is making a lot of money and is affluent, but in reality, she's *adding to her debt* at the rate of $10,000 per year.

On the other hand, Joe makes $50,000 per year, but he only spends $45,000, which means he can *save or invest* $5,000 every year.

After five, ten, or twenty years, who will have a better life? Sally will be facing a mountain of debt, while Joe will have saved as much as $100,000, which he can invest to create a stream of passive income.

This brings us to the subject of your budget.

Budget

Your budget is simply a list with two columns, like a spreadsheet. One column lists your income for the week, month, or year. Most people budget by the month, so we'll use that. The second column lists all of your expenses for the month. *Every* expense—don't leave any out!

Like this:

MONTHLY INCOME	EXPENSES	COSTS
My job $2,400	Withholding	$500
	Rent	$500
	Car	$400
	Food	$500
	Clothes	$100
	Phone	$200
	Savings	$200
TOTAL $2,400	TOTAL	$2,400

This table is very simple and was created on an ordinary Word document. You can also go online and find free home budgeting spread-sheets that have more features.

If you live at home and either work or attend high school, your expenses may be fairly minimal—your phone, perhaps a car payment, some clothes, and personal supplies. This is the perfect opportunity to save your money, and for most young people, the goals of saving are either for college or a house.

If you live in an apartment or have bought a house, you'll have a major expense in the form of your monthly rent or mortgage payment. This is usually the biggest expense you'll ever have, followed by student loans, healthcare insurance (if you pay out of your own pocket), and car payments. It's very easy to become "rent poor," which means that you're paying so much for housing that you have very little left over for other expenses.

The commonly accepted rule of thumb is that you should spend no more than 30 percent of your *total paycheck* on rent. But this rule was invented back in 1969, and because of the amounts of money that are now withheld from the typical paycheck, I personally think this is too high, and you'll be much safer if you calculate your 30 percent on your *take-home* pay. Your take-home pay is the amount you actually deposit in the bank for your immediate use. It does not include money withheld from your paycheck before you get it, which in the U.S. may include:

1. Federal income tax.
2. State income tax.
3. Social Security (FICA).
4. Medicare tax (FICA).

5. Insurance policies.

6. Retirement fund contributions.

7. Other payroll withholdings.

If your paychecks total $2,400 per month, your take-home pay, after amounts withheld, may be more like $1,900, and this is what you should base your budget on—not the higher figure. Therefore, the maximum you should be paying per month for rent or your mortgage should be $1,900 x 30 percent = $570.

In addition, you may have student loan debt, which will further reduce your net pay. Your geographical location makes a difference, too. If you live in a city, you'll have no choice but to spend more on rent than if you live in a low-cost suburb. In one area, $570 a month might get you a nice, sunny one-bedroom apartment, but in another area that same $570 a month might get you a cramped basement studio unit! The high rent you'll find in desirable locations is why many young people start out with a roommate, just like in college. With a roommate, you can double the rent you pay to $1,140 a month, allowing you to get a nicer place.

Income Taxes

By April 15 of each year, the Internal Revenue Service (IRS) requires most U.S. citizens and permanent residents who work in the United States to file a federal tax return if they made more than a certain amount during the previous year. (In other words, in April of any given year you will file a tax return for the money you made in the previous year).

Please note that tax laws are subject to change without notice. Be sure to check with IRS.gov or any reputable tax service such as Turbo-

Tax or H&R Block for current information on this or any other tax topic. There are also charitable tax preparation clinics for low-income people; there might be one in your neighborhood.

You may want to file with the IRS even if you made less than the minimum amount, because you may get money back if you had federal income tax withheld from your pay (very likely!), made estimated tax payments (unlikely), or qualify to claim tax credits such as the Earned Income Tax Credit and Child Tax Credit (possible). You can file your tax return as early as mid-January—check with the IRS for the exact date.

After you file your personal tax return (IRS form 1040), there are four possible outcomes:

1. You'll get a refund from the IRS because more was withheld from your paycheck than you owed. Yay! Your refund can be sent electronically, directly into your bank account.

2. You'll get no refund and owe no money because you've paid your taxes.

3. The IRS will tell you that you *underpaid* and owe more money. If this happens, either pay it immediately or contact the IRS and get on a payment plan. If there is one rule of life that you must know, it's this: *Don't mess around with the IRS.* If you're respectful to them, they'll be nice to you; and if you call the IRS and state you intend to comply and pay your taxes, they are likely to put you on a payment plan and not garnish your wages. But if you ignore letters from the IRS (they always send snail-mail letters), they will take action to collect from you. Unlike credit card issuers, who have little recourse if you fail to pay, the IRS can arrest you and charge you with

tax evasion; and if you're convicted, send you to prison. It's not worth it! If you sincerely believe the IRS is wrong about how much tax you owe, you need to hire a qualified tax attorney to represent you.

4. The IRS will tell you that you're going to be audited. This is rare for middle-income taxpayers. In 2022, a Syracuse University report found that the odds of audit for returns filed by those earning less than $25,000 were 12.7 out of every 1,000 returns filed. But for filers reporting more than $25,000 per year in income, the rate was much lower—only 2.3 for every 1,000 returns filed.[45]

If you get notified you're going to be audited, you can simply "go it alone" and comply with whatever the IRS tells you, or you can hire a tax advisor to assist you.

The vast majority of taxpayers file their income taxes electronically. To prepare and file your Form 1040, simply go online and choose one of the major tax preparation services—TurboTax, H&R Block, TaxAct, JacksonHewitt, Intuit, and others. Open an account, and then just follow the directions. You'll be asked a series of questions that ensure you'll either get a refund or pay the correct amount of tax, or perhaps pay no tax at all.

This is key to remember: The IRS does *not* offer tax preparation services. To compensate for that, by federal law, commercial tax preparation services must offer federal personal income tax filing for free. Most young people who are simply paying taxes on their income from a job can have their IRS Form 1040 prepared and filed for free by any of the commercial tax preparation services such as TurboTax. More complicated tax returns will require a fee.

You may also have to pay state income taxes—in the vast majority of states, you do! Go to your state's government website to check. All of the major tax preparation services offer package deals where they will guide you through your state income tax form, which will be largely identical to the IRS Form 1040 with some variations.

The online tax preparation service will usually charge you a fee for preparing and filing your *state* income tax form. However, many states have programs whereby certain classes of taxpayers can file for free. Be sure to visit your state's Department of Revenue to find out if you qualify for free filing.

Can you file an old-fashioned paper tax return? Technically, you can, but every tax agency implores taxpayers to file electronically. It's much faster and safer, and with a reduced workforce at federal and state tax departments, your paper tax return may languish, unopened, for weeks.

TAKE ACTION!

- If you don't yet have a bank account, save up a small amount of cash—$100 should do it—and open a bank account. You should have both a savings account and a checking account. You must have a bank account in order to deposit your paychecks and any other money you earn or is given to you.

- If you have a smartphone, you probably already have one or more electronic funds transfer apps. Be sure to review the fees associated with them, and be aware of your privacy. Don't agree to any condition where your financial history might be revealed.

- Make a monthly budget using a simple table or spreadsheet you can get for free online. List your income and all of your expenses, including an amount that you're saving. Make sure your expenses do not exceed your income.

- Do not fail to file your federal and state income tax forms! To get your refund, you can usually file as early as mid-January. Check IRS.gov for the most up-to-date information, as well as the Department of Revenue in your state. If you need assistance, explore free tax preparation clinics in your area or consider the help of a qualified accountant to ensure that you file your taxes accurately and on time.

- You can either live at home or in a college dormitory, or rent an apartment. Most young people don't buy houses because they move around too often and it's much cheaper to rent. When renting, make sure you understand your lease. Do you need advice about your lease? Ask your parents or guardians, go to a government or charitable tenants services organization, or consult a lawyer.

- Your goal should be to achieve a good credit rating of 690 or above. This will allow you to access credit when you need it, such as when you buy a car or a house. Check your credit score every month (it's free) and take the necessary steps to correct problem areas that appear in your credit report.

- You can build and improve your credit rating and FICO score by having one or more credit cards and using them very sparingly, and be sure to always pay them off before the due date.

- When using your card, remember that a debit card takes money out of your bank account immediately and offers no fraud protection. A credit card requires you to deliberately pay your credit card bill at a later date, and is likely to offer fraud protection.

- For personalized financial guidance and to stay updated with the latest financial regulations, consider consulting with a qualified financial advisor who can offer tailored advice based on your unique financial situation.

6

College Costs, Loans, and Credit Cards

The borrower is a servant to the lender.

— King Solomon

ortunately, in America and most industrialized nations, public schools are free and kids are able to earn a high school diploma without borrowing money.

If you choose to go to college, that changes. In the United States today, the least expensive choice for a four-year college bachelor's degree education is to attend a local state university. Costs vary from state to state, but according to EducationData.org, as of 2023 the average cost of attendance for a student living on campus at a public four-year, in-state institution was $26,027 per year, or $104,108 over four years. This rate combines the tuition and on campus accommodation fees.

If you can live at home and attend a nearby state school, you'll just have to pay the tuition, which has recently averaged $9,377 and a few additional costs, such as for books.

If you choose a private, non-profit college, the recent average cost is $55,840 per year or $223,360 over four years.

Beware of private, *for-profit* colleges! Some are respectable, while others are "diploma mills" whose business model is to rake in as much federal student loan money as possible. Some of these for-profit colleges have gone bankrupt, so do your research.

You can also earn your college degree either 100 percent online or in a "blended" program where you attend some classes and take others remotely. This can lead to big savings, but the quality of your degree may be questioned.

Okay… but how to pay for college? You have five sources of funds:

1. **Your family.** Maybe your parents or guardians can just write a big check. Lucky you! Of course, this is very rare, but hopefully, they can contribute something. In fact, if you apply for federal student loans, your parents or guardians may be required to make a contribution if they have the means.

2. **You and your job(s).** You can work during the summer, and many colleges have work-study programs where they place you in a part-time job on campus. This can be a big help—be sure to ask the financial aid office at your school about this! (You should become best buddies with the people in the financial aid office. They can really help you.)

3. **Grants.** A grant is money that you don't have to pay back. The federal government, states, cities, and the colleges themselves have grant programs that are usually based on need. For example, the U.S. Department of Education (ED) offers a variety of federal grants to students attending four-year colleges or universities, community colleges, and career schools. They include Federal Pell Grants, Federal Supplemental Educational Opportunity Grants (FSEOG), Iraq and Afghanistan Service Grants (for dependents of soldiers who died as a result

of service in the U.S. military in Iraq or Afghanistan after September 11, 2001), and Teacher Education Assistance for College and Higher Education (TEACH) Grants.

4. **Scholarships.** Like a grant, you don't repay a scholarship. It's a gift. There are thousands of them, offered by communities, schools, private companies, employers, individuals, nonprofits, religious groups, and professional and social organizations. In general, while grants are given based on financial need, scholarships are usually merit based and awarded to students based on their academic achievements, extracurricular activities, or field of study.

5. **Loans.** For most students, loans are a necessary evil. Like a credit card or a car loan, a student loan is money you borrow and must pay back with interest. There are many types of loans, and they can come from the federal government, from private sources such as a bank or financial institution, or from other organizations. Federal student loans usually have more benefits than loans from banks or other private sources. They include:

- The interest rate on federal student loans is fixed. It's usually lower than what you'll find on private loans, and *much* lower than any credit card.
- No credit check or cosigner is required for most federal student loans.
- You don't begin repaying your federal student loans until after you leave college or drop below half-time.
- If you have difficulty making your payments, the government has flexible plans for which you may be eligible.

When you apply to a college and are accepted, the financial aid office at the college will usually prepare a *financial aid package* for you. This is their "best offer," and may be a mix of student loans and grants from the college itself. You'll see exactly how much you'll be paying over four years. Legitimate, accredited colleges and universities *never* increase the cost for students who are already enrolled. When they announce price increases, it's always for incoming students.

If you've been accepted to multiple colleges, you can compare the costs and aid offers. Accept the offer from the school that's best for you.

Federal Student Loans: The FAFSA Form

To simplify the process of applying for financial aid to multiple colleges, in the U.S. the federal government administers the process with the Free Application for Federal Student Aid (FAFSA) form. Each year, you and your parents or guardians fill out the FAFSA form, which asks about your income and net worth, as well as the income and net worth of your parents or guardians. FAFSA sends the info to every college to which you're applying, at no charge to you. The college that accepts you uses your FAFSA data to determine your federal aid eligibility. Many states also use FAFSA data to award their own aid. After you submit your online FAFSA form, you'll receive your Student Aid Report, showing you what you're eligible for.

Please note that at some colleges, the admissions officers will see your FAFSA report, while at others they will not see it. At the 100 or so "need-blind" colleges in the U.S., your application for admission and financial aid are kept separate. While the admissions people can see that you've filled out the FAFSA form, they have no access to the information within it, and must decide to admit you without regard for your financial status.

The majority of U.S. colleges, however, are "need-aware." This means your FAFSA application for financial aid and your application for admission are read at the same time by the admissions officers, and your financial status can be used as a factor in the decision.

The financial aid office at your college will administer your loans and grants, and apply your aid to the amount you owe your school. Any remaining balance will be turned over to you to spend on other college costs.

Student debt can be significant. According to EducationData.org, the average student borrows over $30,000 to pursue a bachelor's degree. The average federal student loan debt is $37,338 per borrower, while student loan debt from private lenders, such as banks, averages $54,921 per borrower. University graduates owe an average of $33,500 upon leaving school, and among student loan holders, the median monthly payment is $250.[46]

Private Student Loans

In order to raise the money you need for your college education, you may need to consider a private student loan. These loans are made by private organizations such as banks, credit unions, or state-based or state-affiliated organizations. Unlike federal loans, which are offered as a public service, private loans are designed to make a profit for the lender. They are generally more expensive than federal student loans, and have stricter conditions attached. Here are some of the key differences between federal loans and private loans.

Interest rates. Federal loans have a low fixed rate. Private loans may have variable rates that can go up. Be sure to read the fine print on your loan agreement!

Cosigner. Private loans usually require a cosigner, who agrees to assume financial responsibility for a loan if you fail to repay it. This creates a risk for the cosigner because they become just as responsible for the loan as you are.

Repayment starts. Federal loans do not require repayment to begin until after you've left school or graduated. Many private loans make you start repaying while in school.

Forbearance. If you must skip one or more payments, federal loans are more lenient. With a federal student loan, if you experience financial hardship, you can take a break from loan repayment for up to three years. Be sure to notify your federal loan administrator and apply for forbearance or loan deferment! In contrast, the hardship protections offered by private lenders vary and are typically granted on a case-by-case basis. Also, private student loans have no loan forgiveness options and must always be repaid in full.

Your credit rating. Private student loans are the same as any other consumer loan, and there's the potential for significant damage to your credit record if you fail to pay them on time. Most private loans will go into default as soon as you miss three monthly payments, while with federal loans, you can miss eight monthly payments.

Subsidized loans. Federal student loans may be offered in "subsidized" varieties. These are only given to students with financial need, and do not accrue interest while you are enrolled. That can reduce the amount of money you need to repay in the long run. Private loans are all unsubsidized, which can significantly increase the overall loan repayment amount.

Repayment based on income. Private lenders don't care about your income; they just want to be repaid. For federal loans, income-driven repayment plans are available that can help you manage your loan by basing monthly payments on your income. This can be incredibly important if you don't earn enough to cover all your bills or you lose your job. Federal repayment plans typically lower your monthly payments and extend the term of the loan.

There are strategies you can use to lower your college costs. Go to a state school in your state, and live at home if possible. Take online courses to earn college credits. And many students are choosing to attend low-cost two-year community colleges to earn college credits, and then transfer to a more prestigious private or state school for their junior and senior years. The savings can be huge, and you'll receive the same diploma as the person who attended the school for all four years.

TAKE ACTION!

- To pay for college, you have a variety of options. Make a plan to put together a package that may include your own money from a job as well as money from savings, family, grants, scholarships, and loans.

- To apply for federal loans, you'll use the FAFSA form. Go to Studentaid.gov and complete the form online. It's free and your FAFSA form will be sent to every college you've applied to. Remember that you'll need financial information from your parents or guardian too.

- Grants are based on need, while scholarships are based on academic achievement. Get busy and research grants and scholarships for which you might be eligible. Because every community has its own resources for local grants and scholarships, you'll have to do your own digging. The best place to start is your high school guidance office.

- When you're looking for money for college, beware of private loans, which are your most expensive option. Focus on federal student loans and other sources.

- Once you're accepted at a college, contact your financial aid office. They will give you advice on how to pay for college as well as administer your account.

7

Your First Set of Wheels

Leave sooner, drive slower, live longer.

— Anonymous

For over a century in America, the automobile has been synonymous with freedom and mobility. You get in, turn the key or push the "power" button, and off you go, either a few blocks to the mall to buy new shoes or clear across the country to start a new life. Your car is not just a way to get from point A to point B; it's an extension of your personality. Do you drive a plain gray "econobox" or a fast sports car? Your family's minivan or a rugged Jeep? An electric car or a gas-guzzling SUV with a big V-8 engine?

I'll bet you have many memories involving cars. Your first long trip in one, or driving yourself to work or school for the first time. You may have yearned for a certain cool car to own, or just thought of them as necessary pieces of hardware to get you where you wanted to go.

You may also have bad memories of cars, such as a terrible accident when you were a kid. Cars can be dangerous; among the leading causes of death among young adults, unintentional accidents rank number one, and the vast majority of those accidents involve automobiles.

Owning a car can be a significant responsibility. After your house mortgage and your student loans, buying a car is likely to be the biggest investment you'll make. In 2023, the average price for a new car was over $48,000! But fear not—the cheapest new cars cost about $22,000, and you can get a good one at that price. If you finance a new car for $22,000 (to "finance" means to pay over time, whereas "buy" means pay the full price when you purchase the item), depending on your credit rating, your payments on a 5-year auto loan will be about $320 a month. You will also have to pay insurance, say $150 per month, plus gas and maintenance, which we'll estimate at $100 per month. So your total cost of financing and owning your economy car will be about $570 a month.

Remember—put this into your monthly budget!

The good news is that after five years you will *own your car*, and if you've taken good care of it, you'll only be paying for insurance and gas and maintenance, or an estimated $250 per month. In the old days, after five years, most cars were rusted out and ready for the junkyard, but today, many cars can accumulate over 100,000 miles with no problems and last much longer than five years. If you want to own one car and drive it until it literally falls apart, then buying or financing a car is your best bet. You finance it, pay for it, and then after five years keep driving it for as long as it will last.

Leasing a car is like renting an apartment—it can work in the short term, but it's not as good for the long term. Car companies and car dealerships love leasing because it's highly profitable for them. They would rather lease you a car than finance a car purchase.

From your point of view, with leasing, you'll have lower monthly payments, all regular maintenance paid by the company, and access to brand-new vehicles. If you're the type of driver who enjoys having a new set of wheels with the latest technology, and you can afford to pay the bill, leasing is a good option. When your lease is up, you may have the option to buy the car, but overall, you'll be paying much more for the car than if you had either bought it for cash or financed it over five years.

The last (or perhaps for many first time car buyers, first!) option is to buy a used car. There are several things to keep in mind when buying a used car. First is, where should you buy? If you have a trusted relative or friend who is willing to part with a car, that can be a solid option. It has the benefit that you know the seller, and can probably track them down easily if something goes wrong. However, money and family or friends are rarely a good combination. When you owe someone you know money, or if they sell you a bad car, hurt feelings can spiral rapidly out of control and damage a close relationship. Consider everything you know about the person selling you the car, make sure you take it to a mechanic for an assessment if you can (if they pressure you not to do that, don't buy it!), and get a notarized contract outlining both parties' responsibilities.

Buying a car from a private seller who is a stranger to you is risky unless you are *very* knowledgeable about cars, have a trusted adult who knows cars, or have access to a mechanic. Even then, experts can be fooled in a variety of ways, and most private sellers may not be willing to let you take the car to a mechanic for an extended check-up. If you *do* decide to buy from a private seller, get a notarized contract just in case. But to be frank, it's not a good idea to buy your *first* car from a private seller you don't know unless, again, you are an expert or can afford fixing it if something goes wrong.

Always be vigilant for red flags such as an exceptionally low price, missing or altered VIN (Vehicle Identification Number), missing or suspicious documentation, or unusual reluctance from the seller to provide proper paperwork about the car's history, as these could potentially indicate a stolen vehicle. Buying a stolen car can lead to serious legal and financial consequences. So, be extremely cautious and ensure all documents are legitimate and verifiable before proceeding with the transaction.

The Federal Trade Commission (FTC) recommends getting a vehicle history report before buying any used car.[47] Go to the National Motor Vehicle Title Information System's website, vehiclehistory.gov, and you'll find an approved list of providers offering such reports. For as little as $10 you can get a complete history of your vehicle, simply by entering the VIN number. A small price to pay for peace of mind!

Finally, there are thousands of used car dealers across the US who will happily finance a used car, especially if you have a cosigner. When buying a used car from a dealership, there are a few things to keep in mind. First, high mileage cars are cheaper, but can be more expensive to maintain. Always check sites like jdpower.com and kbb.com, both sites that rank cars on a variety of metrics, including how safe they are in an accident, any issues they might have, and customer satisfaction based on surveys of actual owners. Last but not least, you want to be sure that the "used" car is cheaper than a new one, as some dealerships will advertise low or no money down, but at the trade-off of having a higher monthly payment and a higher interest rate, both of which can put the price of a used car much higher than buying or leasing a less expensive new car. Remember to use the 5WH^2 method, especially for a purchase as big as a car!

Should You Even Buy a Car?

For many young people, the idea of owning a car may be debatable. The wisdom of owning a set of wheels will depend on four factors:

1. Your commute to work. Can you get to work or school on public transportation, or by walking or biking?
2. Your family responsibilities. Do you have children who need

to be taken from place to place, or are you a carer for relatives who are disabled or elderly?

3. Is public transportation readily accessible to take you food shopping and places on weekends?

4. If you had a car, could you park it easily and cheaply?

If you can easily commute to work or school, don't need to get children or relatives from one place to another, have access to the places you want to go for weekend activities and routine errands, and struggle with parking a car, then owning a car is likely unnecessary for you.

Your alternatives include public transportation (subway or bus), ride-sharing services (Uber or Lyft), taxi cabs, and your own power—walking or bicycling. And increasingly, many urban dwellers are using personal motorized devices including scooters and electric bicycles to get around.

Much will depend upon where you live. For example, New York City has a highly developed public transportation system and relatively few places to park. Across the five boroughs, 55 percent of households do not own a car and only 22 percent of people commute to work by driving alone in a car. Fully 66 percent of all workers commute by public transit or walking.[48]

In contrast, Los Angeles is a sprawling city with a sparse public transportation system. There, you'll find a vehicle ownership rate of 87.9 percent and an average of 1.63 cars per household. Just about everyone drives to work, and the type of car you drive is a direct reflection of your job status and the personality you wish to project to others.[49]

Buying and Operating a Car

It is common in rural areas and on farms for kids to learn how to drive cars and tractors around on private property from an early age.

The law gets involved when you want to drive your car on any public road, from a one-lane dirt road to an interstate highway. Then you need to meet certain qualifications.

1. To simply *drive* a car, you must have a driver's license, and the vehicle needs to be registered and insured. Additionally, you need the owner's permission. Driver requirements vary by state—refer to your state's Department of Motor Vehicles (DMV) website for specific details.

2. To *own* a car and drive it, you need to register it, own the title, and have proper insurance. In most states, you need to be 18 years old to do these things. Laws vary by state, but teens under 18 likely need the help of an adult to put a car they buy on the road.

To get your driver's license, check the laws in your state. Licenses fall into three levels: the learner's permit, the restricted license, and the full license. Ages at which you can get your learner's permit range from 14 to 16. You graduate to your full license between the ages of 16 to 18. Every state is different, but the basic procedure is some form of training ("driver's ed"), actual driving experience, and then a test with both written and road components.

The most important form of auto insurance that you must have, and most states require, is *liability insurance*. This is insurance that you buy which protects *you* in the event you cause an accident in which someone else is injured. Liability insurance does *not* cover damage to your own car or injury to yourself, only damage to others for which you're legally liable.

It's incredibly valuable. Let's say you're driving and you become distracted, and you crash into another person's car, injuring them. The injured person gets a personal injury lawyer (like the ones you see advertised on TV) and they sue you for $100,000. Without liability insurance, you'd be paying that yourself, but with liability insurance, your insurance company will pay it.

When out on the road, most states require you to have, in your vehicle or on your possession, two very important documents: Your driver's license and your vehicle registration. These are the two documents a police officer will ask to see if he or she pulls you over. Best practice is to always keep these documents easily accessible in the glove box—even when you rent or borrow a car. The registration provides the officer with information about the vehicle. It officially certifies that the excise tax has been paid, the vehicle has a license number that matches the exterior license plate, and the vehicle has a listed owner.

In some states, the registration also indicates the vehicle is properly insured. In other states, you'll need to carry a separate document proving you have liability insurance.

If you own your car, you will also have a title. This is a legal document issued by the state government to demonstrate who owns the vehicle. Keep your title in a safe place at home; you'll need it only when you sell your car.

Time for Some Tough Love

You may not want to hear this, but the facts are the facts: As we mentioned earlier in this chapter, if a teenager or young adult dies or is seriously injured, the cause is likely to be from a motor vehicle accident.

According to the National Highway Traffic Safety Administration (NHTSA) publication "Young Drivers Traffic Safety Facts," in 2020, young drivers, while comprising only 5.1 percent of all licensed drivers, accounted for 8.5 percent of all drivers involved in fatal crashes. It's not that young adults are bad people, but that operating a motor vehicle is a complex activity that takes years to fully master. This is why most states have restrictions on young drivers—not to torture them, but to help them stay alive while they hone their driving skills.

The system is called *graduated driver licensing* (GDL), and it's designed to provide young drivers with an opportunity to gain experience behind the wheel under conditions that minimize risk.

First introduced in New Zealand in 1987, it was adopted in Florida in 1996, and has since spread to all U.S. states and the District of Columbia. The systems vary in strength, but the general format is three stages: a supervised learner's period, where you need a licensed adult with you while you drive; an intermediate license, which limits your driving in high-risk situations including at nighttime or with teen passengers; and a regular adult license with full privileges.

When you're first driving alone, play it safe! If you're inattentive for even a moment, an accident can happen.

The Two Keys to Defensive Driving

In any driver's education class, one of the most important concepts is *defensive driving*. It's an important subject worth reviewing.

Defensive driving is the idea that you need to operate your vehicle—car, motorcycle, truck—as if *at any moment* some crazy driver could do something unexpected and dangerous to your safety, or something about the road could change and pose a danger to you, like a huge pothole suddenly appearing as you come around a corner. When unexpected things happen, you need time to respond and avoid the danger. The more time you have, the better chances you have of staying safe. The less time you have, the worse are your chances.

How do you gain time for yourself to respond?

You gain time in two ways.

1. Keep Your Speed Down

At 60 miles per hour, your car is traveling at 88 feet per second. If your car is 15 feet long (the average), it will travel nearly six car lengths in just one second. Researchers say that at 60 mph, a typical driver can stop their vehicle in a total of 6.87 seconds, including a 1-second delay for driver reaction. Your total stopping distance will be slightly over 300 feet—the length of a football field![50]

So let's say you're driving your Chevy at 60 mph in a 35 mph zone. First of all, you're speeding, and if the police see you, they'll stop you and give you a ticket. For a young driver, getting a speeding ticket for going 60 mph in a 35 mph zone is *bad news*. You could have your license suspended and your insurance rate will absolutely go up. Here's why: In most states, each time you receive a traffic violation or cause an at-fault collision, the state slaps you with a predetermined number of driving record *points*. Points are *bad*. They translate into percentage-based additions to your car insurance rate. The more points you have, the more you will pay for insurance. The fewer points you have, the less you pay. The best rates go to drivers with zero points.

Every time they pay their auto insurance bill, better drivers save themselves money.

To get back to our story, you're going 60 mph in a 35 mph zone. You're traveling 88 feet per second, and you need about 300 feet to come to a full stop. Suddenly, 200 feet ahead, you see some guy has stopped in the middle of the road. You think, "What the heck?" and then you think, "I'd better stop!" So your foot goes to the brake. Your car begins to slow down as the other car gets closer.

Too late! You cannot stop in time. You smash into the back of the other car.

You were going too fast. But the outcome could have been very different. If you had been going at the posted speed limit of 35 mph, you could have stopped in just 100 feet and safely avoided the crash.

Why is that? Because the slower your speed, the *rate* at which you can reduce your speed increases, and you can therefore stop more quickly. In contrast, a car going 60 mph has much more momentum than a car going 35 mph, and takes much longer to slow down. For example, this means that if it takes you 100 feet to go from 35 mph to a dead stop, it does *not* mean that it will take you 100 feet to go from 60 mph down to 35 mph. No—it will take you 200 feet, and also much longer in time. Remember this rule: The faster you're going, the longer it will take to reduce your speed.

Having rear-ended the car stopped in the middle of the road, the story doesn't end there. For you, it gets *worse*.

Why? Because the police will conclude that the crash was *your fault*.

With the exception of big highways, the rules of the road say that you must always be able to bring your car to a stop if there is some obstacle in the road. If a pedestrian is crossing, or a utility crew is working, or a school bus has stopped to let kids off, you must be able to stop in time. The posted speed limits on roads are designed to reflect this reality, which is why speed limits in congested areas are always lower than on open roads.

The bottom line is this: Always obey the posted speed limit. It was designed not to torture you but to keep you and others safe.

2. Keep Your Reaction Time Short

How quickly you sense and respond to a problem on the road can mean the difference between being safe and getting into an accident.

You'll remember that in the scenario described above, the researchers included a reaction time of one second. That was probably optimistic, and would apply to a driver who was sober, paying attention, and not distracted. But in reality, many of the people with whom you share the road are very distracted or otherwise impaired, which slows down their reaction time. When you drive defensively, you're ready to cope with the poor skills of the drivers around you.

What can make your reaction time longer?

Many things. Here are just a few.

- Alcohol and other drugs. Blood alcohol concentration (BAC) is the metric used in measuring how much alcohol, in grams, is present per 100 milliliters of blood. A BAC of 0.08 means your blood is 0.08% alcohol by volume. The higher your BAC, the more impaired you are. The lowest rating is .02%, which means you're slightly impaired, while the highest ratings are .31% and up, which can kill you. Federal law has established a legal limit of 0.08% at which point you can be placed under arrest for drunk driving. In addition, states have their own laws, and for young drivers some states have a "zero tolerance" BAC of 0.00%, which is sometimes referred to as a "not-a-drop" law.

If you're in a car accident and you've been drinking, your legal misery will be magnified. The bottom line is this: If you're going to drive, be stone cold sober. If you want to drink and party, then take public transportation, call an Uber, or get a ride from a friend who is not drinking.

- Using your phone. One of the leading causes of accidents is texting while driving. When cell phone use exploded in the early part of this century, states began to pass "distracted driving laws," designed to keep the eyes of the driver on the road. All 50 states have some sort of distracted driving law. They include a ban on all handheld cell phone use, all hands-free phone use, texting, and combinations of these laws for young drivers. In most states, these laws are *primary enforcement laws*, which means that a police officer may ticket you for using your handheld cell phone without any other traffic offense taking place. In other words, if a cop simply *sees you* using your phone while driving, he or she can pull you over and give you a ticket.

- Drowsy driving. Too many Americans of all ages are sleep deprived, and this leads to accidents on the road. According to the National Highway Traffic Safety Administration (NHTSA), every year 100,000 police-reported crashes and over 1,500 deaths are the results of drowsy driving. In addition, it annually causes 71,000 injuries and $12.5 billion in monetary losses.[51]

Drowsy driving mimics drunk driving—the effects are very similar, and include slowed reaction time, blurred vision, and poor decision-making. Some drivers can even experience *microsleeps*. This is when you literally fall asleep and your brain shuts down for a few seconds. Your eyes may even be open, but you're not seeing anything. You can imagine how dangerous this can be if you're behind the wheel of a 4,000-pound car hurtling down the highway at 60 miles an hour!

If you feel like you're nodding off while driving, *pull off the road*. Solutions like playing loud music or opening the window will not help. You've got to *stop your car and get out*.

- Inattention to the road. To have a quick reaction time, you need to have good *situational awareness*. This is a skill that will serve you well in life as a whole, not just driving. It refers to your ability to know what's going on around you, using your five senses—sight, hearing, touch, taste, and smell. When you drive your car, the primary sense you use is sight. If you have good situational awareness, your eyes are always in motion. You're looking ahead, in the distance and close up. You're looking to each side. You're looking in your rear-view mirrors. You're aware of the cars around you and behind you. You see the guy on the side street ready to pull out, and the yellow light up ahead, and the pothole in the middle of your lane, and the driver following too close behind you. If something suddenly appears to be a hazard, you see it instantly.

- Inattention to your vehicle. Listen for unusual sounds—the wail of a siren or even a strange noise coming from your own car.

If you feel the road vibrations, and if your car starts to shake for no reason, this is a signal that you might have a mechanical issue or a flat tire. You may even smell something peculiar that may indicate a problem with your car. Tire "blow-outs" (continuing to drive on a flat tire until the point where it bursts completely) are *extremely* dangerous. They can cause you to lose control of your vehicle. So if you do notice any of these "signals" that something is not quite right, remain calm and pull off the road when it is safe to do so. Check your tires immediately, and if necessary, call for emergency assistance.[52]

- Driving at night. The NHTSA reports that 49 percent of vehicle occupant fatalities occur at night. Given that only 25 percent of travel occurs during hours of darkness, the dangers of nighttime driving are clear. Combine the two stats and the odds of being in a fatal crash are 3 times higher at night as compared to daytime.[53] Many families have lost loved ones due to nighttime driving—and I, myself, have a devastating story to share.

I offer this personal experience not to scare you, but to raise awareness of the very real potential consequences of nighttime driving.

In 2007 I lost a dear cousin, age 40, to an incident of "car-blinding." This is the term for when high beam headlights—in my cousin's case, from an oncoming truck—hit a driver dead in the eye, effectively blinding them. The effects of being struck in the eyes by powerful headlights can lead to disorientation, and an inability to see for 5 to 10 seconds[54]. This can cause you to lose complete control of your vehicle, leading to swerving and even, as was the case for my cousin, running off the road completely.

My cousin, tragically, left behind a pregnant wife and three toddlers. As one grace, the passenger survived, and was able to tell the tale of how the accident had been caused by car-blinding. This is why I am passing it on to you, with the hopes you never experience such trauma.

So, let's be proactive! What can you do to stay safe if you *have* to drive at night?

1. Aim your headlights correctly and clean them often. Help prevent car-blinding by switching *your* lights to low beams when there's another vehicle approaching.[55]

2. If you find yourself in a situation of car-blinding, do not look directly into the lights and try not to panic. Instead, focus your vision to the right edge of your lane. Use that as your guide to avoid swerving. Never put your high-beams on as a response, as this can further blind oncoming drivers and increase the risk of accidents. If a vehicle with high beams on is approaching you from behind, flip your rearview mirror up. This will prevent the light from hitting you directly in the eyes. When it's safe to do so, slow down and pull into a safe space, such as the emergency lane or a gas station. Wait here until your vision, if affected, has returned to normal.[56]

3. At night, reduce your speed to compensate for the limited visibility and extend your stopping distance.[57]

4. Dim your dashboard.

5. If you wear glasses, make sure they are anti-reflective.

6. Clean the windshield often to eliminate streaks.

When you drive your car, motorcycle, or truck, you're moving through a dynamic environment where change can happen very quickly. Situational awareness represents your ability to navigate a fluid landscape and arrive at your destination safe and sound each and every time.

Two-Wheeled Transportation

Depending on where you live, you may be able to commute and get around town on two wheels. It may surprise you to know that in many of the world's big cities, bicycles are more common than automobiles because you can get around faster on two wheels. According to the International Science Council, around 42 percent of households worldwide own one or more bicycles, which is a higher percentage than households with access to a car or motorcycle.[58] Globally, bicycles are more common than cars and are used as an affordable mode of transportation.

Cycling is not only a healthy activity, but it's eco-friendly and sustainable. This is why, in March 2022, the UN General Assembly adopted a resolution promoting cycling to combat global warming. The resolution recommends that all Member States integrate bikes into public transport systems in urban and rural settings, take action to improve road safety, and promote cycling as a mode of transport that reduces greenhouse gas emissions."[59]

In cities, bicycle-sharing systems are growing rapidly. Their development was made possible by wireless technology, and by 2022, approximately 3,000 cities worldwide offered some version of bike sharing. The programs include both docking and dockless systems. Docking systems allow you to rent a bicycle from a special bike rack and return at another node or dock within the system. Dockless systems offer a node-free system relying on smart technology, where you leave the bike anywhere and its location is pinpointed by smartphone web mapping. In July 2020, Google Maps began including bike share systems in its route recommendations.

In addition, electric bicycles (or e-bikes) are becoming affordable and practical. You can buy either an electric bike designed for that purpose, or an add-on kit that you can attach to a regular bicycle. Prices for good quality e-bikes start at around $1,000. Conversion kits are less, but you'll need some mechanical know-how to install them, unless your local bike shop will do it.

You can also buy e-scooters, which start at the same prices as bicycles. The biggest problem with scooters is that they have relatively small wheels, which makes it more challenging for riders to navigate irregular surfaces and obstacles on the sidewalk or street.

Compared to cars and even motorcycles, e-bikes and e-scooters offer significant savings from fuel alone, and the operating costs and the ownership costs for e-bikes are dramatically lower.

With any bike, e-bike, or e-scooter, safety is paramount! Using these alternatives means, you're sharing the road with cars, and trucks. As you might expect, when a crash occurs between a bike (or scooter), and a vehicle, it's the cyclist (or e-scooter user) who is most likely to be injured.

Your number one safety precaution is to wear an approved helmet. When buying a helmet, you must ensure a proper fit so your helmet can best protect you. Take your time to ensure a proper helmet fit, because your life is worth it! Always ride responsibly, and remember that all states require bicyclists to follow the same rules and responsibilities as motorists on the road.

TAKE ACTION!

- As you decide whether to get a car, research other transportation options. You may be better off using public transportation! Investigate public transportation in your area, or think about using a bicycle, e-bike, or e-scooter—with the proper safety precautions. If you're really lucky, you may even be able to walk to work or school!

- Stay proactive and make well-informed decisions! Check local resources, consult experts, and stay informed about the latest updates on driving and transportation. Verify state-specific driving laws, graduated driver licensing regulations, and any shifts in car ownership costs caused by factors like inflation, fuel prices, and insurance rates.

- Take your driver's education class seriously. Don't assume that just because you're smart, you know all about driving. You don't. It takes time to learn.

- Buy or finance a car if you plan to keep it a long time. If you think you'll be trading it in after just a year or two, you might be better off leasing.

- When buying used vehicles, be cautious with private sellers you don't know. And get a vehicle history report for a small fee from vehiclehistory.gov for peace of mind.

- Ensure your driver's license, registration, and proof of insurance are in your car before you hit the road.

- When you drive, keep your speed down to the posted limit. If you exceed the limit, your chances of getting into an accident increase—not to mention getting a ticket.

- Stay alert! Drive sober. Get enough rest. Prepare for the increased dangers of driving at night, such as car-blinding. Anything that impairs your reaction time or your judgment could get you or an innocent person killed. These are worst case scenarios, but ones that could result in a criminal record.

8

Getting Your Own Place

No, this is not the beginning of a new chapter in my life; this is the
beginning of a new book! That first book is already closed, ended,
and tossed into the seas; this new book is newly opened, has just
begun! Look, it is the first page! And it is a beautiful one!

— C. JoyBell C.

*Y*ou've made progress in life and in school. You may have work
experience or you've just graduated from college. Now you're
ready to leave your home or dorm room and live on your own.
Let's review your options.

When your grandparents were at your age, and newly graduated
from school and entering the workforce, they had a clear choice: Buy
a "starter home" or rent an apartment. This was a real choice because
in that generation, a two-bedroom family home was affordable to just
about anyone who had a full-time job.

Times have changed, and the vast majority of young people do
not buy homes. They rent apartments, either solo or with a roommate.
Compared to buying a house, this is the realistic choice for 5 reasons:

1. Young people are highly mobile. When the lease is up after a
   year, they're likely to move.

2. Renting is simpler. When you rent, you know your expenses
   are fixed. You don't have to pay for normal wear and tear on

your unit. Your landlord pays if the roof leaks or the heating system fails. (And if your landlord fails to fix these issues, call your city housing inspector and report the problem!)

3. Buying and selling a house or condominium is an expensive process. There are significant fees involved, which is why you shouldn't do it more than a few times during your entire life. To make a profit on a house, you generally have to own it for several years.

4. Houses are becoming insanely costly. This is not just in terms of the price, but in terms of the percentage of income needed to buy a house. Experts use the *price-to-income ratio* to show how much of your income you need to buy a house. In the 1960s, when your grandparents bought their first house, the ratio was 2, meaning it took two years of average income to buy an average house. Today, that ratio is 3.6, meaning it will take that many years of income to buy a house. This is a huge difference, and points to the fact that personal incomes have not kept pace with the costs of housing. The result is that most young people are postponing buying a house—in fact, the National Association of Realtors reports the average age of the first-time home buyer is now *thirty-six.*[60]

So, if you're like the vast majority of young people, when you move out of your childhood home or dorm room, you will almost always move into an apartment.

In most states, you can legally sign a contract and rent an apartment at the age of eighteen. In a few states, the age is sixteen. There may also be exceptions for emancipated minors and individuals who are married or in the military. If you're not sure, ask your parents, guardians, or school counselor; or go online to find your state's laws; or simply ask the landlord who's renting the apartment you want—if he or she is a professional, they should be familiar with state law.

When presented with a lease agreement by a potential landlord, read it very carefully! Don't let a landlord intimidate you or suggest that "it's just a standard lease—no need to read every word!" Even if you are nervous or feel as though you need to act quickly, be firm and polite and tell the landlord you need to read the lease completely. You may want to show the lease to your parents, guardians, or lawyer. Also, every state offers free online guidance for renters.

Remember that the landlord's obligations to you must be spelled out in the lease. For example, the lease must specify the months or date range that heat and/or air conditioning must be provided. The lease might say, "heat shall be provided for every room up to 68°F from September 15 to June 15."

If an obligation is not specified in the lease, the landlord can later say, "Sorry—it's not in the lease."

Your obligations will be spelled out also—usually relating to payment of rent, other things that you must pay for, not damaging the unit, not conducting any illegal activities, rules about smoking and pets, and so forth.

Your apartment lease is usually for one year. At the end of the year, you and your landlord may mutually agree to renew it, or one of you may decide to let it expire. If you allow your apartment lease to expire, you should suffer no financial penalty.

Here's why. When you sign a lease for an apartment, in most states your landlord can ask that you pay your last month's rent in advance plus a security deposit that's usually equal to one month's rent. This means that if you rent an apartment for $1,000 per month, you'll need to pay $3,000 before you move in: Your security deposit, last month's rent, and first month's rent.

Before you move into your new place, an assessment or inventory appointment will usually be scheduled. This is because apartments are rented and then re-rented quickly, so it's likely that some damage will be present—such as marks left from pictures hung by the previous occupants; or holes drilled in the wall for their smart TV fixtures or Wi-Fi router—pay close attention during this appointment. If your landlord or realtor does not schedule one, *insist on it.* Any pre-existing damage should be carefully logged and you can take your own video or photographic evidence before you move in. Keep a copy of this inventory, which your landlord should sign, along with any videos or snaps—timestamped!—of your own.

When your lease expires and you're going to move out, your landlord is legally obligated to return your security deposit and to apply your last month's rent deposit to your last month's rent. You should know that landlords are notorious for refusing to return security deposits, often citing spurious claims of damage. Before you leave your apartment, take a cell phone video of the entire unit, top to bottom, to show there's no damage in addition to any pre-existing damage that you carefully inventoried before you took occupancy. Nobody wants to be stung with the fees of re-painting an entire wall or repairing drill holes left behind by a previous tenant. Security deposit laws vary by state, so if your landlord hasn't returned your security deposit according to the terms spelled out in your lease, consult your local government agency that oversees landlord-tenant disputes and rental regulations, or a tenants' rights organization, or if you live in an area where such a resource doesn't exist, speak to a lawyer!

Most states have a Sanitary Code that sets the minimum standards for rental housing. You can find your state's code online, as well as directions for how to file a complaint. The code usually covers issues including heat, water, electricity, kitchen and bathroom condition, fire exits, garbage collection, rodent and insect control, lead paint, building maintenance, and the renter's responsibilities.

Most states also have laws preventing your landlord from retaliating against you if you file a complaint.

It's very important to check your state's code. Some states are "landlord friendly" and provide few protections for renters, while other states are "occupant friendly" and provide more protection for you.

The Roommate from Heaven... Or Not...

If you lived in a dorm at college, you already have experience with roommates. You know that a roommate can become your BFF, while another may seem like they were sent on a unique mission to test your patience.

Ideally, you'll be able to rent an apartment with your college BFF and you'll both live happily ever after—or at least until one of you decides to move on.

But in real life, it's likely you'll find yourself with someone who's just an acquaintance, or co-worker, or even someone you met during a roommate search.

If you need to look for a roommate, here's how you can do it safely.

The goal is that you want someone agreeable who shares your worldview and values. If you're a strict vegetarian and the person who wants to be your roommate is very nice and sweet but *lives* for barbecued ribs and chicken kebabs, you're going to have a problem!

If you're stuck and don't have any leads from friends, family, or co-workers, then (as with nearly everything else these days), you're going to go online. Sources include Roommates.com, Roomiematch.com, Padmapper, and Roomster.com. These sites and apps are designed to introduce you to qualified roommates in your area. If they sound like dating sites, the principle is the same: to match two people with similar interests and expectations.

Let's say you're at the point where you're communicating with a complete stranger whom you've met through one of these sites. Now the process becomes very much the same as a job interview. The difference is that you'll be interviewing each other—after all, this person is in the same situation as you. Don't be shy! Ask questions—and be prepared to answer a few yourself, like these:

- What's your work schedule like?
- Do you smoke, drink alcohol, or use drugs?
- What time do you normally wake up and go to sleep?
- How often do you like to clean?
- Do you have any food or animal allergies?
- What do you do for recreation in your free time?
- How often do you have visitors over? Who are they?
- Will you be bringing any furniture with you?
- Do you need a parking place?

Unlike a job interview or the questions a landlord can ask you, when you interview a potential roommate, you can ask *anything that's important to you.* You can ask about their religion and gender identity. You can ask about their politics and worldview. And you should not object if your candidate asks the same questions of you.

However, *never* share your bank account information, wire them money, or accept a money transfer from them. You don't want to put yourself at risk for identity theft or fraud.

When you've met someone whom you like and could make a good roomie, get a few references from their previous landlord or employer. You can also run a background check (for a fee) through sites like First Advantage or E-Renter. You should volunteer to undergo the same process for them.

Unless you sublet to your roommate, both of you will have to sign the lease. But the lease does not cover your agreement *between each other*. Determine whose name is on the utility accounts, and how you will split the bills. How will you share food costs? Is there a "lights out" time each night? Will you permit "sleepover" guests? Who will clean the bathroom? Figure out these details early on so there are no surprises when you're sharing the same four walls and locked into a contract. In fact, you should write a separate roommate agreement so everyone is on the same page.

As for little conflicts that may arise, it's just like any other personal relationship. Keep your cool, be empathetic, but look for clarity. Try not to let differences fester.

If your roommate becomes toxic, and gets physically or emotionally abusive toward you, *don't be a victim*. If you feel that you are in danger, call the authorities right away. Pack up and seek immediate safety and support, whether it means reaching out to a trusted friend or family member, contacting a local domestic violence hotline, or finding a safe shelter. Start looking for alternative housing options. Even if you have to break your lease and lose your deposit, get out. Money can be replaced—but you are precious and irreplaceable!

Those Empty Rooms Need Furniture and Some Plants!

While you can occasionally rent a furnished apartment, the vast majority of apartments are rented with just "four walls," meaning there is no portable furniture. The items you'll typically find in an apartment are fixed utilities including the bathroom fixtures (toilet, sink, shower and/or tub) and the kitchen fixtures (stove, refrigerator/freezer, sink). There will also be wall outlets for electricity, central heat, possibly air conditioning, and possibly an internet connection. Before you sign a lease, be sure these fixed components are clearly listed and meet your state and local codes.

Now you need furniture. Well, to be precise, you need as much furniture and other items as you envision. Some young people just throw a futon on the floor and get some milk crates to make a table, and call it a day. But if you want an apartment that you can live in comfortably, you have several sources to furnish it.

1. Your childhood home. Your parents or guardians may let you borrow extra furniture, kitchen equipment, rugs, bedding, lamps, electronics—whatever they don't need. Free stuff!

2. Thrift stores. These were traditionally where young people shopped for home furnishings. It might be the local Goodwill or Salvation Army store, a second-hand store, or an antiques store. Second-hand stores are very common in college neighborhoods because students are highly transient and buy and sell furniture regularly. However, when purchasing used furniture, be cautious about the potential presence of pests such as bedbugs or other insects. Thoroughly inspect any items you plan to buy, and consider treating them or consulting a professional if you have concerns about pests. Being vigilant about this aspect can help ensure a bug-free and enjoyable experience with your second-hand furniture.

3. Online resellers, such as eBay, Facebook Marketplace, Chair-ish, Kaiyo, AptDeco, and Etsy, are good sources for used furniture in every price range.

4. IKEA. In the past few decades this Swedish global retailer has captured the market for inexpensive, durable, attractive home furnishings that—famously—you assemble yourself. The self-assembly feature is a major reason why their prices are low. For years, IKEA did not deliver, so you had to find a way to lug your "flat pack" cartons home. Today, many IKEA stores deliver, and you can also shop online.

5. Online retailers. You can also scour online retailers including Nordstrom, Target, Pottery Barn, Crate & Barrel, Costco, Home Depot, Sam's Club, Amazon, and Walmart. Some are premium and sell fine furniture, while others have lower price points for young people on a budget.

Begin by determining which items you should buy new and which ones you can buy used. Generally, personal items including bedding and towels you'll either bring from home or buy new. Most people also buy a new mattress for the bed. (If the bed has a mattress, ask your landlord about that. Old mattresses can be difficult to dispose of.) Anything else that you can wash thoroughly, such as dishes, you can buy used, as well as most large items like chairs.

Decorating an apartment can be fun because there are no rules—you can create the environment you want! You might be the type of person who wants an environment that's super-simple and uncluttered, with just a few choice pieces. Quality over quantity, as they say. Or you might be a collector who feels comfortable surrounded by lots of knick knacks. You might have a few cherished childhood items, like your favorite teddy bear, plant, or movie poster. You might want to lug as much stuff from your family home as your parents or guardians will let you. Again, if you're paying the rent, it's your choice. As time passes, you'll learn what you need and want.

As for me, although I'm not the best at caring for plants, having them in my first apartment made a significant difference in creating a welcoming place and promoting a positive state of mind. At first, I had difficulty keeping them alive, but eventually, I discovered indoor plants that survived alongside me and became loyal companions. So here are some suggestions of easy-to-maintain plants: snake plants, spider plants, jade plants, aloe vera, and pothos. For those who prefer flowers, I recommend petunias, geraniums, and begonias—although these need exposure to daylight, so placing them near a window is best.

Home Security

When you live on your own, you're responsible for your own security. It's a sad fact of life that crime exists, both in cities and rural areas, and you need to take the appropriate steps to keep yourself and your apartment safe.

One thing you can do before you rent an apartment is go online and check the crime rate for your potential neighborhood. You can enter a Zip Code and see the various rankings of the area. Bear in mind that high crime rates tend to lower property values and rents, so in a safer neighborhood you may see higher rents for similar sized units.

Also, visit the neighborhood at night. Do you feel safe? Are there people around or is it deserted? Do you see anything like drug trafficking going on? Ask yourself, if I came home at midnight, would I feel safe?

Here's a ten-point checklist for your apartment safety.

1. Install a security system. Many home security companies offer products with renter-friendly solutions like adhesive attachment and wireless connectivity.

2. Upgrade your door lock. There are many ways to improve the locking system on your door and windows. A door security bar or door jammer is a common device that's angled between the center of the door and the floor for extra reinforcement, making it nearly impossible to break down the door.

3. Use window locks. You can add locks that prevent the window from being raised more than a few inches. Keep your doors and windows locked whenever you leave your apartment.

4. Reinforce sliding doors. If your apartment has a sliding door, a common solution is to place a metal or wooden rod within the bottom door track that prevents the door from being slid open.

5. Close the curtains at night. Don't give potential criminals a free preview of you and your stuff.

6. Take out renter's insurance. An insurance policy will cover the loss of your personal property. Some apartment complexes and landlords may even require a renter's insurance policy as part of the lease agreement.

7. Store valuables in a safe in your apartment. Consider bolting it to a wall or floor for extra protection against theft. If you don't need to access a valuable item very often, keep it in a safe deposit box at your local bank branch. You'll pay an annual rental fee, but it might be worth it.

8. Know your neighbors. Take the time to meet those who live

around you. One of the best deterrents to crime is neighbors who know and look out for each other.

9. Give the illusion you're home. If you will be away from your apartment for an extended period of time, create the illusion that you're home by using a timer to turn on a light or TV while you are away. It's easy to program a smart TV or your home security system to do this.

10. Don't post on social media anything about your address or when you're home or not home. Thieves and criminals look for such information and exploit those opportunities. Insurance companies may also check this information on social media. If you're away for an extended period, your policy might not cover losses or damages that occur during that time. To prevent this issue, review your renters' or homeowners' insurance policy.

11. If you think you're being followed home, go to a public place instead and call a friend, or call the police if you feel threatened.

Tidy Up!

I don't want to lecture you about housekeeping, but you'll find that keeping your stuff organized will save you time and reduce your headaches when you want to get out the door in the morning.

Here's an example. If you have a car, you've got a key fob and probably a spare. Where do you keep your car key when you're at home? In a jacket pocket? On the table? In a purse? Wherever you happened to toss it last night?

How many times have you frantically searched for your car key?

There's an easy way to solve that problem. In some obvious place, like the kitchen wall. Whenever you come home, hang your car key in that same spot. After a while, the habit will become second nature. You can hang your apartment key there too. You'll never have to hunt for your keys again. Speaking of car keys, did you know that you should *never* keep your smart key near the front door or windows? Thieves can intercept the key's signal from outside, and then use the data to open and steal your car. A simple way to prevent this is to store your smart key away from exterior walls. Placing it (and any spares!) in a metal box, an everyday object such as an empty coffee can, or a signal-blocking pouch (also known as a Faraday bag) provides the highest level of protection—quite literally "foiling" any interception attempts![61]

To enhance time management efficiency, extend that same attitude toward your entire apartment by maintaining a well-ordered living space. Picture those stressful moments when you're running late and desperately searching for a specific shirt or pair of slacks. Keep your closet and bureau organized and make it easy on yourself!

Maintain a healthy environment by regularly dusting and vacuuming. You can get an inexpensive "stick" type vacuum that doesn't take up much space. If you get a canister model, you won't have to worry about buying bags.

Never, ever leave dirty dishes on the kitchen counter. It's gross and invites pests such as ants, roaches, and flies. If you don't have a dishwasher and you've simply got to leave in the morning, then at least rinse them off before leaving them in the sink to wash later.

Get a hamper or laundry bag for your dirty clothes. There's nothing immoral about tossing your dirty clothes on the floor; it's a matter of personal pride, mental discipline, and practical convenience. Hampers also help reduce the "dirty laundry" smell in a home and make it easier to know when it's time to do the next load.

TAKE ACTION!

- Before interviewing a potential roommate, prepare a list of questions that are important to you—and be prepared to answer the same questions in return. Be sure to write up an agreement between yourselves specifying each person's responsibilities.

- Be aware of your personal security. If you find an apartment you like, before you sign a lease, visit the neighborhood at night and observe the activity.

- When presented with a lease agreement by a potential landlord, read every word of it. Do not hesitate to show it to your parents, guardians, or lawyer. You can also get free online guidance for renters in your state.

- Most states have a Sanitary Code that sets the minimum standards for rental housing. Check your state's code and know what you're entitled to.

- When visiting an apartment, be accompanied by a trusted adult or a friend who has already done that and who can give you advice. Two opinions are better than one!

- To furnish your new place, you can raid your childhood home, visit thrift stores, go to IKEA, and scour online sellers.

- Make your shopping list. Determine your needs vs. wants and prioritize your purchases according to your budget. What do you want to buy that's new? Probably personal stuff like pillows and towels. What can you consider as used? This will be something washable and less personal like dishes, chairs, used clothes, or an appliance like a TV. This will help you figure out where to buy the items you need—Facebook Marketplace vs. IKEA.

- You can take steps to enhance the security of your apartment. Be sure to check with your landlord before making any changes to the locks or other equipment that is the property of the landlord. Make the landlord verify the locks have been changed and the previous renter doesn't have the same key.

- Take the time to meet your neighbors. You can look out for each other!

- Don't post on social media anything about your address or your personal schedule, such as when you're going on vacation. Post your vacation photos *after* you return home.

- Keep your place tidy and organized! You'll feel better and waste less time looking for your stuff.

9

Food, Glorious Food!

Tell me what you eat, and I will tell you who you are.

— Jean Anthelme Brillat-Savarin

Taking ownership of your food choices is one of the most important practical aspects of transitioning into adult life. According to Statista,[62] in 2022, 89 percent of Millennials and 73 percent of Gen Z adults prepared meals at home. So it's likely that you will be spending time in the kitchen too! And cooking for yourself, or for friends and family, can be one of the great joys of adulthood.

Maybe you've been cooking for years, and have a wealth of experience; maybe you never learned, and have relied on your parents, guardians, or even your school to choose and provide the food you eat. If the latter, then even the simplest food preparation can be a daunting task to take up. This section is designed to help you explore your options, and make your new culinary world as easy to navigate as possible.

So, regardless of your previous experience, you're now on your own to fend for yourself. There are three major factors that will influence your choices regarding your food preparation:

1. **Your experience and confidence in the kitchen.** If you're an old hand at cooking, you'll step right into the role with ease. A few years ago, a 21-year-old student at Columbia University

named Jonah Reider operated a "restaurant" (to use the word loosely), named Pith, in his dorm room. Reider charged $10 to $20 for five- to eight-course dinners, serving a maximum of four people per night, that he prepared in his dorm's common kitchen. At one point, he had a waiting list of several weeks.

You may be at the other end of the scale, and barely able to push the right buttons on your microwave to make popcorn properly. That's okay—I'm sure you have many other skills!

2. **Your work schedule**. You may have time to spend half an hour in the kitchen in the morning and evening, making your own food, and perhaps for your roommate too; or you may have a hectic, unpredictable schedule that leaves little time for food preparation.

3. **The availability of fresh foods.** Jonah Reider lived in an area where he could easily shop for quality ingredients. Sadly, many areas of our nation are classified as "food deserts." This is defined as a region—usually low-income urban or rural— where residents have few to no convenient options for securing affordable and healthy foods, especially fresh fruits and vegetables.

As a mother myself, this chapter espouses the information I'd want my own daughter to have when moving forward into the challenging and exciting world of food preparation. I cannot offer specific advice on such a broad topic as nutrition, and I'm certainly no expert chef, but my hope with this chapter is to offer constructive, general advice that can help you build the tools you need to explore food on your own.

The first, best, and most important advice I can offer is this: fed is best. A healthy diet is important, but what is healthy for you may be very different from those around you. As you take up the task of feeding yourself, remember that food of any kind is better than no food or not enough food. In their *StatPearls* study "Nutrition and Hydration Requirements in Children and Adults,"[63] authors Unaiza Faizan & Audra S. Rouster calculated that adults need between 2000-2800 calories a day. While there are recommendations about what form those calories should take, and a lot of advice about how and what you should eat to be healthy, the first and most critical thing is that you should eat *enough*.

Explore Your Neighborhood Food Sources

When you rent an apartment or buy a house, one of the very first things you should do is scout out the nutrition landscape in your immediate neighborhood. You need to find out your options and how you can buy or make healthy meals.

Identify the local grocery stores and supermarkets. Hopefully, one or more are within a few minutes of your place. Find out whether they deliver and their hours of operation. Most supermarkets are open late at night, or even 24 hours, to accommodate working people.

You may have online choices. Instacart.com is an online aggregator, meaning they link to dozens of supermarket chains across America. Or you can go to the supermarket websites directly, like Wal-Mart and Kroger, and place your order for pickup or, in many cases, same-day delivery.

There are also meal plan services like HelloFresh and EveryPlate, where you can subscribe to receive ingredients for home-cooked dishes.

You select the dishes you want to prepare, and they deliver a weekly package with pre-prepared ingredients and easy-to-follow recipes for each dish. While these services may seem pricey, around $8 per serving, it's worth weighing this cost against other factors—like food waste, time, transportation to and from the store, and the availability of affordable grocery stores with similar quality ingredients. If you find it overwhelming to shop for and prepare dishes yourself, then meal plan services can be a lifesaver.

Regardless of how you get your groceries, don't forget to use coupons! They may seem old-fashioned, but the coupons that supermarkets provide in newspaper inserts and online can save you real money. Don't hesitate to use them. And some retailers, such as CVS, give you lots of coupons with your receipt. Be sure to look them over!

You can also use price comparison apps like Reebee. You enter the name of the product you want to buy, like cherries, and it shows you the price of cherries in different stores. If your grocery store follows a price-matching policy, you can ask them to sell you the cherries at the lowest competitor's price!

Don't Be Ashamed to Ask For Help

So, you're out on your own, and the time has come to prepare your own food. What do you do if you have no idea what to make? What if there's food you *want* to make, but have no idea how? What if you simply cannot afford food? Or what if you're among the 40 percent of Americans with a digestive disorder?[64]

For these, and many other problems surrounding diet, there are a variety of options. But first, it's important to note: there is nothing shameful or wrong about asking for help with food.

Services like the Supplemental Nutrition Assistance Program (SNAP), formerly known as "food stamps," are there to be used. According to the Pew Research Center,[65] "On average, 41.2 million people in 21.6 million households received monthly SNAP benefits in the 2022 fiscal year." Of those adults receiving benefits, almost 10 percent had a Bachelor's degree or higher, and 24 percent were employed the entire time they received benefits. Despite frequent rhetoric to the contrary, 63 percent of SNAP users are white, and 87 percent were born in America.

If you find yourself in the position to need SNAP benefits, you are not a failure, you are not taking resources from those in greater need, and using benefits has no bearing on your personal worth. The programs are there *specifically* to help those who cannot afford to eat. Should you find yourself choosing between food and other bills, or consistently unable to eat enough, Google your state name and SNAP. Requirements vary from state to state, and may change as often as every year, so be sure to read the application guidelines carefully. If you're not sure you qualify, *submit an application anyway.* Each state maintains hundreds of people whose sole job is to determine if an applicant is qualified. It costs you nothing to apply, and you might be surprised to find out you qualify.

If your application is approved you will be issued an Electronic Benefits Transfer (EBT) card that you use with an assigned pin, inconspicuous from other methods of card payment. Almost all major grocery stores such as Walmart, Target, Aldi, Costco, and Trader Joe's accept EBT cards as a form of payment. Pharmacies like CVS and Walgreens will also accept this payment for eligible *food* items. Amazon has even partnered with the U.S. government to enable you to link your

EBT card to your account and use your funds for groceries in most states[66]. As for local stores, check for commonly posted signs at the entrance stating "EBT Accepted."

As with SNAP benefits, food banks can be a life saver, especially if you only need help sometimes, don't qualify for SNAP, or have recently applied for SNAP and are waiting for your application to be processed. If for some reason you can't get to the food bank, there are mobile food banks in many areas which will deliver the food to you. The USDA's most recent numbers indicate that in 2020, almost 7 percent of households in the US used food banks.[67]

Asking a Professional

But what if the question is not "how can I eat?" but "what should I eat?" For most young people, the question of diet is a confusing morass of pop culture diets, eating habits engrained from childhood, recommendations from friends and family, and personal preferences. Personal preferences are especially important in light of research that suggests that you may have better, healthier outcomes if you eat what you enjoy. In a 2020 study published in the mega-journal PLoS One, Alexandra Bedard et al found that depending on how you classified enjoyment, people who enjoyed eating food experienced better nutrition than those who viewed food as an unhealthy, guilty pleasure.[68]

On a personal note, I follow the Mediterranean diet for myself and my family, drawing inspiration from the ancestral culinary traditions of the Mediterranean people. This diet, with its associated health benefits, gained recognition in the American context due to the work of physiologist Ancel Keys, who studied it in the 1960s. While Keys played a crucial role, the diet's increasing popularity was also credited to the collective efforts of various scientists and health advocates. Keys continued to advance his research, eventually presenting the diet to English-speaking audiences in his influential 1975 publication, *"How to Eat Well and Stay Well the Mediterranean Way,"* [69] which further solidified its place in American dietary culture.

The beauty of the Mediterranean diet lies in its focus on overall eating patterns rather than rigid prescriptions. This flexibility allows individuals to embrace its core principles according to their unique preferences and needs. The main aspects of this diet include a focus on plant-based foods and healthy unsaturated fats like legumes, olive oil, fruits, vegetables, and whole grains such as whole-wheat bread and brown rice. It also encourages moderate consumption of fish, dairy products (mostly cheese and yogurt), and poultry, with occasional servings of red meat.

Since it's linked with lower risk factors for heart disease, the diet is recommended by American nutrition experts, and recognized by the World Health Organization (WHO) as a pattern for healthy eating. [70] That's why I encourage you to consider it as an option.

One question still remains—what food is healthy for *you?* As best practice, when in doubt, ask a professional! There is an entire specialty of medical professionals who study diet, known variously as Registered Dieticians, Registered Dietician (Nutritionist), Licensed Dieticians, and Licensed Dietician (Nutritionist.) All four of these titles are interchangeable, but ensuring that the professional you see has one of these four titles is key. If you're struggling to determine a healthy diet for yourself, these experts can provide you with medically sound, individualized, research-backed advice to help you determine the healthiest way to eat.

You *do not want* to go to a "Nutritionist" or "Wellness Coach" or any other "professional" that claims to offer dietary advice. Many of these individuals are completely uncredentialed and can only offer advice based on personal experience. *Especially* if you have a medical disorder that requires diet to treat, or if you are experiencing symptoms related to eating or disordered eating, these unqualified, unregulated "nutritionists" can be very dangerous. If you need to speak to a medical professional about your diet, or want to embark on a plan to improve your diet, ask your general practitioner or family practitioner for a referral.

One final note is that if you suffer from diabetes, you may want to further narrow your requirements to a professional that is a Certified Diabetes Educator (CDE). All CDE's are registered or licensed dieticians, but not all dieticians are certified to treat diabetes. The bottom line is, if you are concerned about a healthy diet or suffer from a medical condition, when in doubt, ask an expert!

If you want to be more conscious about what you're consuming, there are apps on hand for most things! Remember Yuka, Think Dirty, and Detox Me from chapter 2, "Self-Care"? Well, these have a double functionality. Just as you scanned the barcodes of your favorite lotions and potions for beauty and self-cleansing, you can likewise use these apps for packaged foods. The ingredients will be explained, a safety rating will be issued, and you'll find yourself well-informed about what it is you're putting in your body for sustenance. If a particular product's safety-rating is low, the apps will offer healthier alternatives that you can scout the shelves for. It bears repeating that these apps do not, and cannot, dispense medical advice, so take what they say with a dose of caution.

Basic Cooking Skills

So, you now know that you can reach out for help to obtain food and to determine what would be best for you to eat. The big question that remains is, "how do I prepare the food?"

Resources abound, but before we begin, let's answer a basic question: Why do we cook some of the foods we eat? After all, there are plenty of foods we eat raw or uncooked, such as many fruits and vegetables. Animals don't cook, so why should we?

Two reasons:

1. Food may be contaminated with harmful microbes that can cause disease. Most experts say that your food needs to reach an internal temperature of 165°F to kill all microorganisms. This is very important!

2. Cooking makes many foods easier to digest, improving their appearance, texture, and flavor. For example, humans cannot digest raw grains; they *must* be cooked before consumption.

Cooking is based on balancing two factors: *heat* and *time*. In general, the more heat you apply, the less time you need to cook an item; but if you "slow cook" at a lower temperature, you can also safely cook your food.

Here are four basic stovetop cooking skills to get you started. Please remember this is not a cookbook, but a very basic introduction to the subject. If you're interested in developing your cooking skills, you can find countless recipes and tutorials online from every culture, as well as plenty of cookbooks. And be sure to refer to Appendix 1 for a list of the top 20 cooking utensils you'll need in your kitchen.

1. Boil an egg.

It's pretty simple, really. You bring water to a boil in a sauce-pan. Gently lay a few eggs in the boiling water. It's possible one will crack—that's just the way it is. For soft-boiled eggs, cook for 4 minutes. For medium boiled, make it 6 minutes, and for hard boiled it's 9 minutes. Use the alarm app on your phone if it helps. You can also buy a thermometer gizmo that looks like an egg, and which you put into the boiling water with your eggs. The egg thermometer will change colors and indicate to you if your eggs are soft, medium, or hard boiled.

When the eggs are done, take the saucepan and pour off the boiling water into the sink. Immediately drench the eggs in cold water. Many chefs use ice water. This will stop the cooking and also make the eggs easy to peel.

2. Fry an egg.

Boiled eggs not your style? Frying an egg is super simple. Just take out your saucepan or skillet and turn on the burner. If your skillet is non-stick, you won't need to put any lubricant in it. If it's cast iron, aluminum, or copper, you'll need to add some cooking oil or butter. Heat the pan. If the oil starts smoking, it's too hot and you should let it cool a bit. If the butter starts splattering and popping, that means the brand of butter you've bought contains too much water. The next time you buy butter, look for a brand with a higher fat content. Crack an egg and drop it into the pan. It should sizzle a little bit. You can leave it there until the yolk is firm. This is called "sunny side up." Or you can flip it and cook the yolk directly on the heat. This is called "over easy."

You can cook it as long as you like—some people like the yolk runny, while others like it very firm.

Since an egg is a good source of protein, for a balanced meal you'll want to serve it with a complex carbohydrate, such as a piece of whole wheat toast, and some fruit, like a banana.

3. Boil pasta.

Once you've mastered the art of boiling an egg, you can graduate to boiling pasta, which is a staple starch of millions of people. When you buy pasta, look at the ingredients list. In classic plain pasta there should be just one ingredient: Durum wheat flour, also called semolina. Egg noodles have eggs, and for color and flavor various other pasta varieties include vegetable juice (such as spinach, beet, tomato, carrot), herbs, or spices. As you probably know, pasta comes in a wide variety of shapes with Italian names—spaghetti, fettuccini, farfalle, pappardelle, fusilli, macaroni—as well as angel hair and many others. It's all the same stuff, made from wheat flour. Some pasta, like ravioli, has a filling of cheese, spinach, or meat.

To cook pasta, boil a generous amount of water in a pot. Put the pasta in the pot. Cook for as long as the directions say on the package, stirring occasionally. For firmer pasta (*al dente*), cook for a shorter time; for softer pasta, cook for a longer time. Simply take out a piece, allow it to cool for a moment, and taste it. If it's too firm, cook for another few minutes.

Put a strainer or colander in the sink and dump the water and pasta into it. Be careful of the hot water! Gently stir or shake to remove the excess water. Add butter or olive oil if desired. Serve either plain with a bit of basil, cheese, or with a sauce. The possibilities with pasta are endless!

4. Pasta sauce.

You're going to need a nice sauce to go with your pasta! Before you begin, you must understand there are countless ways to make spaghetti sauce. Every chef has his or her own version, and each culture has its own tradition. They have names—Marinara, Alfredo, Bolognese, Pomodoro, Carbonara, and so forth. There is no right or wrong—there's only what you prefer!

You can use prepared pasta sauce, of course, but be sure to read the label if you have any allergies—or scan with one of those helpful apps if you simply want a health rating!

Making your own is simple, and if you make a big batch you can refrigerate or freeze what you don't use. A simple Marinara sauce generally consists of canned tomatoes (crushed or pureed), onions, garlic, and herbs. In a pot with olive oil, simply chop the onions and sauté them over low heat until they're brown and translucent. Keep stirring them! Then add some crushed garlic cloves and quickly brown them (don't burn them!). Then add your tomatoes, salt, and pepper, and a bit of dried oregano if you wish. Again, keep stirring the pot. Simmer the sauce for about 15 minutes, allowing the flavors to meld, and take it off the heat. When it's warm enough to serve, stir in some chopped basil leaves, and serve your delicious, homemade sauce over pasta. Add shaved Parmesan or Romano cheese to enhance the flavor. You can also supplement with a side of salad to ensure you eat as many fruits and veggies per day—your body needs these to stay healthy! This should take you no more than 20 minutes to prepare. You can also add a protein such as browned ground beef or cooked shrimp. Many chefs add sliced mushrooms to the mix as well—toss them in the pot after the onions and before the garlic.

You'll notice that I haven't written this in the form of a recipe with exact measurements. If you ever watch cooking shows, you'll note that most stovetop dishes don't have written recipes. The chef just says, "Some of this, a pinch of that. Cook until done." It's all about the feeling!

In contrast, baking is all about *precision*. If you bake anything, you must *follow the recipe exactly*. Baking a cake or a loaf of bread involves a series of delicate chemical reactions, and the slightest variation can ruin the whole thing. Do not try to improvise!

5. Cook rice.

Use 1 measure of rice (such as a glass, a cup, or ½ cup), along with 2 measures of water (or chicken broth, or coconut milk). Add a small amount of fat to prevent sticking (butter, olive oil, vegetable oil). Cover the pot with a lid and simmer over medium heat for 15 minutes or until the water is completely absorbed. Remove from heat and add the sauce of your choice—even the same sauce you use for pasta!

Unleash Your Inner Chef!

Now, how do you go from basic skills to preparing delicious food that satisfies and nourishes? You can, of course, search YouTube for cooking tutorials, or Google recipes and follow along. The downside, of course, is that the quality of these resources can vary and figuring out which YouTube chef and which recipe site or blog knows what they're doing can be time consuming and frustrating.

My personal recommendation is chef Ricardo Larrivée. A beloved Canadian television host and a food writer. In 2002 he created his own TV cooking show, *Ricardo*, shot in his home kitchen in Chambly,

Quebec. It became the longest-running cooking show in Canada, and by 2023, it was broadcast in 160 countries. In addition, he launched a cooking magazine.

Ricardo has written many books and has his own website. Since 2016, he has operated a restaurant, Café Ricardo, in the greater Montreal area.

To the great disappointment of his millions of fans, on April 20, 2023, Ricardo announced that he would be leaving the TV kitchen after 21 seasons and nearly 3,000 episodes.

Of course he's on YouTube (who isn't?), and there you can find many of his easy-to-make recipes and tips on cooking.

You can also visit his website at ricardocuisine.com, which features over 7,000 recipes and 4.4 million monthly visitors.

I love his recipes because they're delicious and nutritious, but most importantly, they're easy to make. You don't need to be a professional chef to succeed with them.

Personally, when I want to learn a new recipe, I visit Ricardo's website or a YouTube channel (if I want to see the execution), and I try the ones that inspire me the most. Because I'm not that passionate about cooking, the ones I add to my favorites are the ones I succeed with on the first try!

There are also apps such as MyFridgeFood or EmptyMyFridge that allow you to tell the app what ingredients you have, and the app will suggest a recipe that you can make with what you have on hand. Websites (or apps) like AllRecipes.com or America's Test Kitchen can also help you with ideas from the very simple to the very complex.

Another resource that often gets overlooked is your local library. More and more libraries offer digital access to their catalog, including thousands of cookbooks, cooking magazines, and more. While personally, visiting the library and getting my hands on a hardcopy book gives me pleasure, there's no reason to stand on tradition!

Last, but certainly not least, local community centers and technical schools often offer low or no cost classes to learn how to cook, both walking you through the basics, and classes covering specific recipes or cuisines. Googling "cooking classes near me" will give you a starting place, or locate your nearest technical school or community center and either request a catalog of classes or search their online catalog if they have one.

Food Storage and Handling

Many foods are attractive to dangerous bacteria. If you ingest bacteria-laden food, you can become quite sick. The effects can last several days until your body expels the contaminated material.

Sometimes the effects of bacteria and mold (another toxic contaminant) are obvious—the food will seem rancid or slimy. But sometimes they're almost imperceptible, so if a refrigerated food item doesn't smell fresh, discard it.

Some foods will last for a long time in your pantry. They include dried pasta, rice, salt, sugar, oatmeal, and any baked cracker or pretzel product in the appropriate airtight container. Canned foods and foods in jars have a long "shelf life." Every packaged food item should be marked with a "sell-by" or expiration date. Check this date and discard any food item that's past it.

Don't forget to clean the inside of your refrigerator. E. coli, salmonella, and other pathogens can contaminate your food before you refrigerate it and get on the racks or sides of your refrigerator. To minimize bacterial growth, keep your refrigerator temperature below 40°F.[71] Regularly clean the inside with soap and water. For a deeper clean, follow by disinfecting with a paper towel soaked in a mild solution made up of 1 tablespoon of liquid bleach per 1 gallon of water.

Wash your fresh fruits and vegetables! Their surfaces or skins may contain harmful germs that can make you sick, such as salmonella, E. coli, and listeria. According to a study by the Environmental Working Group, 75 percent of non-organic fresh produce sold in the U.S. potentially contain residues of pesticides. This is extremely serious as the CDC (Centers for Disease Control and Prevention) has linked pesticide contamination with increases in miscarriages, birth defects, and developmental disabilities in children.[72]

When preparing your produce for eating, risk-free, begin by ensuring your hands, kitchen utensils, and food preparation surfaces are clean, including chopping boards and countertops.

To get rid of any contaminants, wash or scrub your fruits and vegetables under cold running water. Do this even if you do not plan to eat the peel, such as with bananas, oranges, and melons. Just get in the habit of always washing them. Rub them gently with your hands or use a commercial vegetable scrubber. Washing them with soap, detergent, bleach, or any other disinfecting products is *not recommended*. Dry the produce with a clean paper towel.[73]

One product that is highly recommended for washing fruits and vegetables is ordinary baking soda, which comes in the familiar little cardboard box.

In a mixing bowl or your kitchen sink (be sure it's clean!), add 1 teaspoon baking soda to every 2 cups of cold water. Submerge the fruit or vegetables in the baking soda water, and let soak for 12 to 15 minutes. Swish the produce around in the water to ensure all sides of the produce are being cleaned. Remove the produce from the water and let dry thoroughly before preparing or eating.[74]

To eliminate odors and keep your food fresher longer, be sure to keep an opened box of baking soda in the refrigerator and one in the freezer.

Some packed items including spinach and lettuce might say they've been washed. It doesn't matter—wash them anyway! For example, in 2019 an outbreak of E. coli contamination was discovered in packaged Romaine lettuce originating from the Salinas Valley region in California. Many people across the country got sick—fortunately, there were no deaths[75].

Food poisoning occurs when you consume food or water that contains viruses, parasites, bacteria, or the toxins made by germs. Most cases are caused by common bacteria such as staphylococcus or E coli. Symptoms include stomach cramps, diarrhea, fever, or nausea a few hours after eating. Often simply vomiting up the bad stuff will make you feel better. Generally, food poisoning is uncomfortable, and you will feel better in a day or two. The main treatment is to drink water to make sure your body does not become dehydrated. Some types of food poisoning can cause serious complications, so if you feel sick, promptly seek medical attention.

Save Those Leftovers!

In the United States, approximately 40 percent of all food is wasted, with about one-third of that waste coming from households.[76] While more than 42 million Americans face hunger each year—including 1 in 6 children[77]—those of us fortunate enough to have food sometimes discard it in the dumpster. Key reasons for wasting these precious resources include buying too much and letting it spoil, cooking in excess and not consuming it, and forgetting about leftovers.

If you want to avoid food waste, either for budgetary, personal, or ecological and societal reasons, here are some tips you can follow.

First, buy only what you know you're going to eat. Perishable purchases should be considered carefully. If you know you can use it before the sell-by date, or you're looking to experiment and try something new, absolutely buy it. But if you're buying to try it, make sure to buy a small portion! On the other hand, it's fine to buy non-perishable foods, like flour and nuts, if you can store them properly.

Prepare only what you can eat. This is pretty easy if you live alone, but it can be challenging if you're cooking for a group. Use your best judgment. Remember though, that "only what you can eat" does include properly stored meals prepared in advance. If you want to eat spaghetti bolognese for a week, make enough spaghetti bolognese for a week and store it properly.

If you make more than you planned for whatever reason, and if you live alone or with a trusted roommate, save your leftovers. If you're going to do meal prep or save leftovers, make sure you have enough storage options. Containers can be bought online or in stores and you can select depending on your budget.

A high quality way to save food is glass storage containers with lids that seal. Cheap or mid-range plastic containers degrade when you store acidic and some fatty foods in them, and if the food you've stored in them goes bad, they are almost impossible to sanitize. Glass sanitizes very well and will last for years, as opposed to plastic containers that will need to be replaced often. This makes glass a very eco-conscious choice as it will save on plastic waste. In fact, the cost of replacing plastic containers often outstrips the cost of buying glass ones very quickly!

If you want to go low-cost and fuss-free, disposable storage bags are very inexpensive. You can choose specialized bags just for freezing, or general bags for snacks, and so on. These bags are available in convenient sizes, such as snack-size, pint, quart, and gallon. Disposable bags are great for busy lifestyles. They are easy to fill, carry, and store, and take up less space in your fridge or freezer for pre-prepared meals. Although not as eco-friendly as glass, or reusable plastic containers, if you make the effort to separate your trash properly, these plastic bags *can* be recycled, and they reduce your water-usage through cutting down on your need for dish- and container-washing.

Back to the subject of leftovers, here's a secret you may not know... Many cooked foods taste better the second time around! The flavors have time to mingle, and when reheated, they come together and become extra delicious. In particular, the sugars in complex carbohydrates can break down further and be released, and the proteins in meats will also break down, making the meat softer. Instead of being a waste item, many people treasure leftovers as a delicacy.

Finally, mark all your leftovers with the date they were put in the fridge. According to the Mayo Clinic, leftovers can be stored in the fridge for a maximum of four days safely, after which the chances of food poisoning begin to climb.[78] If you don't think you'll eat it in four days, or if you plan to save it for longer, or simply if you're unsure, store it in the freezer. While food in the freezer will keep far longer, it's still best to go through your freezer once a month and throw out anything that's been in there for 3 months or longer. Reheat frozen leftovers to 165 degrees, and if you choose to thaw them first, use the microwave, store it in the fridge overnight, or submerge it in cold water in a sealed container.[79]

TAKE ACTION!

- Remember the Golden Rule of nutrition:

- *Fed is best. Try to eat healthy, but the most important thing is that you eat enough.*

- Don't be afraid to ask for help. SNAP and food banks exist to make sure that everyone has enough to eat. There's no shame in using them.

- When you move into your new place, quickly identify the local grocery stores and supermarkets, as well as your online choices. Consider things like price comparisons, coupons offered, cost of transportation, and quality of ingredients.

- Learning some basic cooking skills saves you money, helps you feel more in control of your diet, allows you to sample a range of foods, and to eat healthier. Now that your food choices are no longer dictated to you by parents, guardians, or schools, make the best choices you can depending on your budget and the foods available to you in your environment. Embrace this essential skill as part of your new freedom!

- Consider the Mediterranean diet. It's simple, inexpensive, flexible, and comes with proven heart-health benefits. The recipes are easy to find online, so explore them for fun and experimentation. Your taste buds might be pleasantly surprised!

- Buy or borrow from home a set of basic kitchen equipment. They won't last long, but in a pinch, you can get everything you need from a dollar store or thrift store. Then, slowly replace your bargain kit with new items over time. Remember to sanitize second hand equipment and *never* buy wooden or bamboo utensils secondhand! They host bacteria and contaminants from previous use, posing health risks. See Appendix 1 for a list of 20 Kitchen Essentials!

- Begin with simple projects like making eggs and boiling pasta, and expand from there. Watch YouTube videos or take classes at your local technical school or community center to learn the basics! *America's Test Kitchen* is also a great show for the basics of cooking.

- Make a list of your favorite recipes. Check out popular chefs like one of my favorites, chef Ricardo Larrivée, and learn from their free tutorials, use the library to download or check out cookbooks. Download apps that let you enter the ingredients you *do* have and then tell you what dishes you *can* make with them.

- Remember the rules about proper food storage and handling. You don't want to get food poisoning! Wash your fruits and veggies in a solution of water and baking soda.

- Try to avoid wasting food. Make only what you'll eat and save those delicious leftovers.

- If you have any doubts about what's healthy to eat for you, consult a Registered Dietician, Registered Dietician (Nutritionist), Licensed Dieticians, or Licensed Dietician (Nutritionist.) to get medically sound dietary advice. Do not go to a "nutritionist" or "wellness coach" for dietary advice, as they are not regulated, licensed, or even trained. If you have diabetes, you may need to see one of the above specialists who is also a Certified Diabetes Educator.

- While cooking for yourself is important, eating out when you can afford it, are too rushed to cook, or just want something special or different, should be a pleasure and not a source of guilt. We all need to treat ourselves sometimes.

But do remember: fed is best!

10

Staying Safe

Safety isn't expensive, it's priceless.

— Anonymous

When you move away from home and live on your own, your safety and security become your own responsibility. You may already have experience watching out for yourself, or this challenge may be new to you. Either way, keep reading for valuable insights!

In discussing this important Actionable Life Skill, this chapter will take a gender-neutral approach. Everyone needs to be careful! But if I lean more towards a woman's point of view, I ask you, if you're a guy, to keep reading to develop empathy and think about the safety of the important women in your life, like your sister, girlfriend, or mother.

In your everyday life as an independent person, you'll face the possibility of various threats to your peaceful existence. To know them is to be armed against them!

Crime

In today's world, crime is all around us. It can happen indoors and outdoors, but often there is an overlap. Street crime takes place in public outdoor locations like vandalism, car theft, mugging, pickpocketing, purse-snatching, and graffiti. Burglary, by definition, takes place inside. But general assaults, drug-dealing, and sexual assault can happen both indoors and out.

Domestic violence tends to occur "behind closed doors," and its hidden nature and the taboo can sadly make victims unwilling to come forward. Fortunately, help is available, including resources such as the National Domestic Violence Hotline. Regardless of gender, if you are currently experiencing domestic violence of any kind, *please* dial 1-800-799-7233, or Google your state domestic violence hotline. You *are* strong enough to break the cycle!

Let's face it—there's a gender gap at work in society when it comes to crime. If you're a woman living alone, you'll experience the threats from the world around you in a way that most men will never understand. Research has documented that, in general, women are more concerned about their personal safety and feel as though they must take more safety precautions than men. The largest disparity exists around sexual violence: Surveys have shown that while the majority of women greatly fear being sexually assaulted, less than a quarter of men say the same.[80] While both men and women fear burglary and getting mugged on the street, women find the prospect of a physical attack more worrisome than either a burglary or mugging.[81] Having said that, women are more likely to be assaulted or killed by someone they know, according to the United Nations Office on Drugs and Crime, while the vast majority of homicide victims are men, killed by strangers.[82] No matter who you are, you should take common-sense measures to keep yourself and your home safe.

Common-sense measures

At home, never open the door unless you are absolutely certain who it is. If you have a peephole, use it. You may also want to invest in a home security system that shows you who's ringing your bell. In an apartment building, be careful about people knocking on your door claiming to be a repairman or plumber. In most states, your landlord or their representatives cannot enter your apartment without providing 24-hours advanced notice. If you're unsure, deny the person entry. If they were legitimate, the worst that can happen is that your landlord will call you to complain. On balance, this is okay!

When walking in a public space, display a confident attitude. Walk with your head up and stay alert. Body language says a lot. Don't look like an easy target! Be aware of your surroundings and other people. If you feel uneasy, walk into a nearby store. If you are concerned you are being followed, cross the street. If the person you are worried about crosses too, repeat. If they cross with you again, this can be a danger sign. Call a friend or trusted person and get to a well-lit, public place asap. If you really feel threatened, dial 911. It's better to be safe than sorry.

Be cautious with strangers who ask for directions or money. They may have an accomplice who will try to rob you while your guard is down. To deter pickpockets and purse-snatchers, keep a secure grip on your purse, bag, suitcase, or backpack, holding it close to you. When using crowded public transport during rush hour, such as a packed bus, train, or subway, ensure that the closures (zippers, snaps, buttons, or any other types of fasteners) face your body. This simple precaution makes it more difficult for potential thieves to access them, reducing the risk of theft.

If you feel threatened, do not hesitate to bring attention to yourself and any potential criminal by yelling. You may also want to carry a whistle or, if legal, a self-defense item like pepper spray. Be sure to check your state government website before purchasing any such devices.

At a restaurant, never hang your purse or bag on the back of your chair and never leave it unattended—if you go to the restroom, take it with you. Wallets should be in a pants pocket or an inside pocket of your coat.

According to the Rape, Abuse & Incest National Network (RAINN), a shocking statistic reveals that 1 in 6 American women have been the victim of an attempted or completed rape in their lifetime. Even in the post #MeToo era, fears over not being believed, facing retaliation by their partner, experiencing societal shame, and self-blame deter many victims from speaking out.[83] This type of violence has lasting repercussions, with many women reporting long-term post traumatic stress disorder (PTSD), higher drug and alcohol use, and relationship difficulties.

While not all cases of date rape involve drink-spiking with drugs like Rohypnol, there is a higher risk in any situation where alcohol is involved. Date rape affects a staggering 35 percent of women aged 18 to 24 in the U.S. and comes with the serious risk of unwanted pregnancy and STDs transmission.[84]

Because extreme vigilance is crucial for personal safety, regardless of gender, never accept a drink from someone you don't know, and never leave your drink unattended. If a drink leaves your line of sight, even for a few seconds, do not consume it, as it only takes this *very brief* moment for a drink to be spiked. Additionally, the drugs that these predators use often impair short-term memory, making it difficult for the victim to recall the details of this hideous crime and accurately report it. This doesn't mean date rape should not be reported— It *must* be reported; *always!* Be aware of the seriousness of this offense, the ease with which one can fall prey to it, and the calculated tactics used by its perpetrators to avoid being caught.

If possible—and especially if you go clubbing at night—bring one or more friends. There's safety in numbers, and you'll probably have more fun!

When Mr. Wonderful Turns Into Mr. Terrible

Dating and then entering into a relationship with a person should be wonderful and fun, but for some women it can get ugly. In some relationships, the man—who may have acted like Prince Charming on the first few dates— may start to show a violent or controlling side. He may start to exert emotional control, and demand to know where you're going and whom you're seeing. He may insist on examining your phone while refusing to let you see his. He may whine about you not paying enough attention to him. He may repeatedly send you flowers to your workplace to compensate for unacceptable behavior (the vicious cycle of abuse: acting out, followed by apology or gifts, then hit repeat).

He may become angry for no good reason, and may threaten you or even hit you.

If any of these things happen, *drop him immediately!*

Do not debate with him. Do not try to "fix" him. Do not listen to his plaintive apologies. He's waving a big red flag in front of you. Do not ignore it!

Yes, it can be painful and scary to remove a toxic man from your life. Maybe you're afraid of being alone, maybe you've become used to destructive co-dependency—but deep down, you *know* you're worth more than this. That you deserve happiness and safety. The longer you let a bad situation continue, the worse it will get. End it, quickly! As Gloria Gaynor sang it loud and proud: You will survive!

Cybercrime

While the many varieties of cybercrime may not seem as physically threatening as getting mugged, they're increasing and—unless you're living "off the grid" in a remote cabin in the woods—can make your life truly miserable.

Cybercrimes are defined as crimes that target or use a computer or a group of computers on the internet for the purpose of harm. They can target individuals, business groups, and even governments.

Having grown up in the information age, you might be rolling your eyes right now, and tempted to skip this section entirely. But you should be aware that cybercriminals target people under 25, and that in 2021, young adults surpassed seniors as the most at risk age group for falling victim to cybercrime.[85]

Here are the major types of cyber threats and how you can protect yourself from them.

Ransomware, Malware, and Spyware

Ransomware is a form of extortion, and it often targets computers used for work, not just personal ones. Criminals demand a ransom payment to halt the malicious actions they've taken on your computer, which often involve wiping out or encrypting all of your files. One of the most significant ransomware attacks in history was the "Wanna-Cry" incident in May 2017, which affected over 300,000 computers in

150 countries and resulted in damages as high as four billion dollars.[86] This deeply sinister attack appeared to have motives beyond profit—it aimed to cause widespread disruption on a global scale.

Malware, which includes viruses, is another category of computer attack where a piece of harmful software is installed on your computer for malicious purposes. Your infected computer, often referred to as a "zombie computer," can be exploited by criminals to send email spam or distribute infected software, without exposing the perpetrator. Millions of zombie computers exist worldwide, with around one-fourth located in the U.S.[87]

Spyware is malicious software designed to clandestinely gather information about you and transmit it to another entity, posing a threat to your privacy.[88] The data collected by criminals may include your usernames, passwords, websites you visit, downloaded files, payment details, and the content of your emails. Spyware operates in the background and is typically invisible unless you possess the technical skills to pinpoint its presence.

To protect yourself from these threats, it's crucial to install a reputable cybersecurity program that offers real-time protection against advanced malicious codes. Affordable brands you may be familiar with are Bitdefender, Norton, MacKeeper, and McAfee.[89] If you suspect that your personal information has been compromised, contact your local police department for assistance.

Identity Theft

Identity theft involves acquiring another person's personal or financial information to exploit their identity for fraudulent activities. The thief can use your personal information and your good credit score to apply for more credit in your name, or make transactions and purchases without your knowledge, ultimately damaging your credit score. You may not find out that a crook is using your name until you begin to get calls from unknown creditors demanding payment for items you never bought!

Identity theft costs as many as 40 million Americans an estimated $40 billion per year in money losses alone, not to mention the headaches and damage to the victims' life. "It's devastating to read impact statements from identity fraud victims," said John Buzzard, lead fraud and security analyst for Javelin Strategy & Research, "especially people who say things like, 'After my identity fraud experience, my accounts were overdrawn, and I couldn't pay my utility bills or buy food.'"[90]

One key to identity theft is your Social Security number (SSN), a unique, unduplicable identifier that you received at birth. Because many companies and organizations ask for your SSN—legitimate workplaces have to, so that they can pay you and have your taxes withdrawn—you should know the laws that relate to who you should and shouldn't give this number to.

Federal law mandates that state tax authorities, departments of motor vehicles, welfare offices, and other governmental agencies can request your SSN as proof that you are who you claim to be. The Privacy Act of 1974 requires that government agencies at the local, state, and federal level disclose to you whether submitting your SSN is required, details on the use of this information, and what law or authority requires its use.

As for businesses such as banks, insurance companies, and credit card companies, they are free to request your number and use it for any purpose that does not violate a federal or state law. If you refuse, they can then refuse to provide you service. You aren't legally required to provide your SSN to businesses unless one of the following is true:

1. You're initiating a financial transaction subject to federal Customer Identification Program rules, or,

2. You'll be engaging in a transaction that requires notification to the Internal Revenue Service.

Skimmers

A skimmer is any electronic device that captures your credit card information surreptitiously while the card is being used for a legitimate purpose. They are most commonly found on ATM machines, and are attached in front of, or underneath, the real card reading device. You insert your card to make a transaction, and while the ATM machine is capturing your data for the transaction, the skimmer is doing the same thing. Sometimes the thief must return to the ATM to collect the skimmer and download it, but some skimmers can transmit data by text, so the thief never has to risk showing up in person. Now the thief has your card information and can make purchases or get cash withdrawals until you or your bank discover the crime.

Servers at restaurants have been known to use hand-held skimmers. They take your card and ring you up, and at the same time steal your card information. In 2011, a ring of skimmers was broken up in New York City. As *The New York Times* reported, a ring of at least twenty-eight servers at exclusive steakhouses including Morton's, the Capital Grille, Smith & Wollensky, and the Bicycle Club skimmed credit card data to then buy "cases of vintage French wine, Louis Vuitton handbags, Cartier jewelry and even a Roy Lichtenstein lithograph of Marilyn Monroe."[91] The thieves were clever—because big credit card bills weren't unusual for these wealthy diners, many were unaware that their information had been stolen.

Phishing Scams

This is when you get an email or text message claiming to be from someone you know, a business that you trust, a government agency, or other sources. They ask you to click on a link (or button) or view an attachment that downloads a malicious software to compromise your computer. Their ultimate goal is to trick you into giving up personal information (identity theft) or financial information to commit financial fraud in your name.

Phishing attacks have become increasingly sophisticated. It's the most common type of cybercrime, with the FBI's Internet Crime Complaint Center reporting more incidents of phishing than any other type of computer crime in the most recently released statistics from 2022[92].

What can you do to protect yourself? Inspect your emails carefully! They are not always what they seem. Typically, phishing emails have these characteristics:

1. They contain grammar errors, misspelled words, or just look unprofessional. However, with the rise of AI, scammers can craft very sophisticated, convincing emails.

2. The subject line may appear enticing or alarming: "Congratulations! You've won…", or, "Unable to deliver your package…"

3. They convey a sense of urgency: "Immediate action required: Your email account will be deactivated…"

4. They include a link or attachment and ask you to click on it: "If you don't validate your information, your account will

be closed within 3 days. Click on the link below…" Be cautious—clicking the link may lead you to a fraudulent form seeking personal information, and simply opening the attachment could infect your computer.

Above all, if you suspect an email might be a scam, do not click on any links or download any attachments. Instead, hover your cursor over the sender's name without clicking on the email. A tooltip will appear, revealing the actual email address of the sender. For instance, the sender's name might be "Bank of America Customer Service," but the tooltip could display something like "bdjsiel2derer@omd.of." Pay attention to the domain name (what comes after "@"); if it's not the official one for Bank of America "@bankofamerica.com," it's a malicious email!

If your email platform has a "Report" button (often represented by a shield icon), click on it to prevent emails from suspicious senders showing up in your inbox. If you don't have this option, delete the email without opening it and consider using a more secure email provider.

If you're not sure whether the email is legitimate, contact the supposed sender through safe means. For example, if you get an email from your bank prompting you to click a link, delete the email and log into your bank account online. Check for any notifications within your account or call the bank's customer service number from their official website (*do not* use any information in the suspicious email!).

Remember, your bank or government agencies like the IRS will never ask you to click links or buttons, or download files, without you initiating a request; instead, they'll ask you to log into your account and view the notification they sent. They may also use snail mail or ask you to visit their website or call customer service.

A variation of phishing is "vishing" (voice phishing), where scammers make automated phone calls to large numbers of people, and then claim to have spotted fraudulent activity on the victim's account. The victim is then prompted to enter sensitive information or manipulated into revealing personal details by a real persuasive person.

If you receive a suspicious call, hang up immediately. Never share personal, financial, or sensitive information over the phone, even if the caller claims to be from a legitimate organization. Instead, look up the official contact information for the organization (e.g., from their website or official documents), and contact them to confirm if the call was genuine. If not, share your experience with family and friends to raise awareness about these types of scams. Keep a close eye on your financial accounts for any suspicious activity. If you suspect your personal information has been compromised, take appropriate measures: change your passwords, call your local police department, and notify your financial institution.

Be equally cautious at work, as many companies make the headlines because of phishing attacks involving employees who accidentally click on malicious links.

Psychological Fraud

Also known as social engineering, this type of fraud refers to the scams used by criminals to nurture and then exploit your trust in order to obtain money or confidential information to enable a subsequent crime. Social media is frequently used, but it is not unusual for contact to be made by telephone or in person.

The most common type of psychological fraud is used against older people. The fraudster calls on the phone and, with a scratchy-sounding connection, claims to be a nephew or grandchild. They claim to be in prison overseas and need bail money sent as soon as possible. The victim—grandma or grandpa—wires them the money. Because you're young, this may not happen to you directly, but it could happen to an elder in your family. You can do your part by not posting family information on social media, and save your vacation posts until after you get home.

Stay in touch with your elders! Let them know they should call you immediately if they get a mysterious call from someone claiming to be you.

Other scams include calling you and saying there's some problem with your bank and you need to wire money or you need to buy a store card and send it to someone.

"Can you hear me?" scams are popular.[93] Here, your phone rings and the caller ID shows it's a local call. You're curious, so you answer.

A voice says, "Hello? Can you hear me?"

You innocently reply, "Yes."

Now the scammer knows two things: The number they called has a real person who will answer it, and they have you on tape saying, "Yes." Scam artists have been known to use a recorded "yes" to claim that the person authorized charges to his or her credit card or account![94]

As laughable as these schemes seem to be, enough people fall for them to make them profitable for thieves.

Financial Fraud

Financial or investment fraud is defined as the illegal providing of false information to someone so that they will invest in something.

Never *ever* trust investment ads circulating on social media. Scammers use social media to find new victims. The ads are so well written that you'd think an economist had crafted them! They even hire actors to shoot videos, testifying about their financial success after dealing with a particular investment company. This fraud is so sophisticated that anyone who isn't careful enough can fall victim to it.

One big red flag is when the fraudster insists that you need to "act fast" and that "time is limited." No legitimate investment company will ever put pressure on you to invest quickly.

Before engaging with an investment firm, be sure to contact your state's financial regulatory authority to check if the company is authorized to operate in the United States. If the firm operates in an unregulated sector (such as cryptocurrency) and claims that's why it's not accredited by the financial regulatory authority, *run away* before they take all your hard-earned savings!

The US Securities and Exchange Commission (SEC) investigates allegations of Internet investment fraud. The SEC encourages citizens to submit any tips, complaints, and referrals (TCRs) using the SEC's online TCR system and complaint form on the SEC website.

The Fake President Fraud

The "fake president fraud" is a variation of financial fraud in which scammers impersonate a company's president, or high-ranking managers such as the Chief Executive Officer (CEO), or Chief Financial Officer (CFO). They target employees who are authorized to make wire transfers of money from the company's account and order the employee to make a cash transfer to a third-party account owned by the criminal. They use persuasive tactics to put pressure on the victim, and may say it's for a confidential deal or some other urgent, secret purpose. And because the employee willingly makes the transfer, such crimes are considered fraud and are *not* covered by cyber crime insurance policies.

Remember to always double-check any strange requests. Talk to your supervisor or use official communication channels to validate the transaction's legitimacy. This way, you'll protect yourself and your company from falling for this deceptive ploy.

The Number One Rule of Social Media

The number one rule of social media is this: If you post a bit of personal information, the entire world—all 7 billion people across the globe—can get access to it.

So, before you post anything about yourself, ask, "Do I want some sketchy dudes in an overseas Internet scam office to see this? What can they learn, and what harm can they do?"

If your Facebook account's password is your date of birth (which should never be the case!) and you post a birthday cake on your birthday, this information may be collected by malicious individuals whose mission is to sweep up such golden nuggets and use them against you.

As a result, your Facebook account can be hacked. You may get a notification about a change to your username and password that you didn't make. Messages you didn't write may be sent from your account, friend requests may be sent to people you don't know, or posts you didn't create may appear on your timeline.

Again, be equally cautious at work! Scammers can be very active on platforms like LinkedIn and Facebook, gathering professional and personal information on individuals working in sensitive sectors to hack their accounts and harm the organizations they work for.

Unfortunately, we live in an era where hackers are sometimes employed by governments to harm others. So, stay vigilant and avoid sharing anything that could compromise your well-being, your family, or your company.

TAKE ACTION!

- At home, never open the door unless you are absolutely certain who it is.

- To lower your chances of being a victim of crime, be vigilant. Be aware of your surroundings and other people. Avoid dark and isolated streets.

- Keep a secure grip on your purse or bag, especially on crowded public transport. Don't hang it on the back of your chair in a public place, or leave it unattended.

- When you go clubbing at night, go with friends in a group.

- In any public setting, or when drinking around people you don't trust wholeheartedly, keep an eye on your drink, someone could put a *date rape drug* in it. If you go out clubbing, try to do so with at least one friend—you will have fun and be able to watch out for each other.

- If you're a woman and your new boyfriend is the slightest bit aggressive or intimidating to you, drop him immediately and block his phone. No excuses, no second chances.

- If you get a suspicious email, never click a link or download a file. Mark the email as phishing, spam or junk and delete it without opening it. ***

- Protect your computer against viruses and purchase well-known antivirus software such as Bitdefender, Norton, McAfee, or MacKeeper. It's an investment that will pay-off in the long term.

- Take password security measures. Check online resources on how to create strong passwords, such as password-monster.com. These free and easy to find online resources will tell you how long it will take a hacker to crack them (a few seconds or thousands of years?).

- Never use your bank account password to secure another account (e.g., your email account). Doing so may compromise your bank account security because the provider of the other account could potentially access it without your consent or store it in an insecure (unencrypted) way.

- Activate two-factor authentication on your accounts whenever available to increase their security level. Typically, you'll need your password plus another factor (face ID or a code sent to your phone) to log into your account. A password is like a toothbrush, it's personal!

- Use a secure connection like your home Internet or LTE to handle sensitive tasks like bill payments, bank transactions, or private emails. Public networks, like those in coffee shops, restaurants, and airports, are not safe. Hackers can easily intercept your personal information on these unsecured networks.

- When charging your devices in public places, avoid public USB ports and use only ordinary electrical outlets with an adapter. Hackers can exploit public USB charging ports (juice jacking) to load harmful software onto connected devices. If you must use them, consider buying a data blocker to prevent data transfers while charging your device and protect against potential threats.

- Be vigilant about your personal finances. Know where your credit cards are. If you give your credit card to a server at a restaurant, keep track of it. Check your balances and charges frequently. Most banks offer protection against fraud and identity theft.

- On your credit card accounts, set your account to notify you by email every time your card is used for a purchase over a certain amount, such as $25. It may seem annoying to get those email alerts each time you use your card, but if you see a suspicious transaction, you'll know right away. Call your card issuer and report the fraudulent transaction. Your bank will likely cancel the charge so you're not liable. They will also cancel your card and send you a new one in the mail to prevent any future threats.

- Take advantage of the fraud protection programs offered by credit reporting agencies. For example, Equifax offers a program that provides alerts of key changes to your Equifax credit report. Dedicated ID restoration specialists can help you if your identity is stolen, and theft insurance plans can help to pay certain out-of-pocket expenses due to fraud.

- If you've been the victim of identity theft, place a fraud alert on your credit report. Close out all accounts that have been tampered with or opened fraudulently. File a report with your local police department, and report the identity theft to the Federal Trade Commission. You should also call the non-emergency line of your local police department and report it.

- *Before* engaging in business with an online company, such as investing in cryptocurrency, contact the state's financial regulatory authority in which the company claims to be operating and confirm that the business is legitimate. You can also use websites like OpenCorporates to check the business's registration status. They should always be registered to operate in the U.S. You can also do a Google search for the company and see what comes up. Often a search will yield hits from victims of crooked companies. On a government level, do a Google search to find details of your state's Cybersecurity Resource Center. All states have one.

- If your Facebook, Instagram, Twitter/X, LinkedIn, TikTok, or any social media account has been hacked, immediately go to that platform's website for directions on how to correct any damage done by the hacker, and to get your account back under your own control.

11

Spirituality and Morality

I have learned that as long as I hold fast to my beliefs and values—
and follow my own moral compass—then the only expectations I
need to live up to are my own.

— Michelle Obama

In the very first chapter of this book, I invited you to look into the mirror and ask, "Who am I?" I did this because it's much easier to make progress in life when you engage in self-awareness and self-reflection. Using these processes in tandem, as we discussed, will help you make decisions based on your conscious goals and aspirations— not just some vague or spontaneous impulse that could be here today and gone tomorrow.

Of course, your job in life is to become the very best version of yourself. As Ralph Waldo Emerson wrote, "The only person you are destined to become is the person you decide to be." Every person has their own path to follow, and in doing so you become a responsible and contributing member of society.

Each one of us—you and me and all of us—need to work together to make the world a better place for ourselves and for future generations. While it may sometimes seem like we live in a world where it's every person for themselves, since the dawn of time, we humans have survived because we have learned to cooperate and work together for the common good.

Think back to thousands of years ago when humans first became dominant on earth, and our physical attributes at that time, which we still have today. Unlike many creatures, we have neither sharp claws nor sharp teeth. We cannot run particularly fast. We have no natural armor, no camouflage. We cannot see particularly well in the dark and we have unexceptional hearing.

So how have we achieved such success? It's the result of our ability to unify around a common goal. We have learned to share responsibilities. In those ancient times, some hunted and gathered while others stayed home to nurture their defenseless children. Some stood guard at night while others slept on the ground, vulnerable to an attack by a wooly mammoth. Some learned to cultivate food while others made clothing.

Because our groups included individuals with diverse personalities and skill sets, it became imperative for us to come together under a common foundation of fundamental morals and spiritual beliefs, not necessarily religious in nature. But the underpinnings of all religions are those bedrock values that unite us and allow us to cooperate with one another.

Trust is the bottom line. At the end of the day, all of our transactions, deals, and partnerships depend upon our ability and willingness to trust both ourselves and the people with whom we choose to associate. When John says, "I will stand guard tonight while you sleep," we need to believe him and trust that he will not fall asleep, or even rob us while *we're* sleeping. When an online store says, "Send $100 and we'll send you the pair of shoes you want," the transaction is based on trust. And when you say to your boss, "I'll write that report for you by end of day today," she needs to trust that you'll get it done.

There are penalties for broken trust. If John dozes off while on guard duty, the village might be attacked by mammoths. If the online store fails to send your shoes, you can take them to court as well as leave a scathing online review for others to see. If you fail to turn in your report as promised, your boss will no longer trust you with important tasks—and if you keep breaking your trust, she may fire you.

Compassion is another important human trait. This is our gift for being able to see the world through the eyes of another person and understand their point of view. Only then, through an informed position, can we take action to relieve their suffering.

If you see that John is dozing off while on guard duty, compassion allows you to go to him and say, "Are you tired? Do you want me to take over for a while?"

If the online store fails to send your shoes, compassion will make you call them and say, "Is there a problem? Are the shoes out of stock? Can I get a refund?"

If you fail to turn in your report, and your boss is compassionate, she will say, "Did you forget? Are you overworked? Can I get someone to help you?"

The opposite of compassion is indifference. The indifferent person will say, "I don't care about your problems. It's a dog-eat-dog world, and only weak people care about others." This may seem like an exciting, "no nonsense" attitude, but if you look at thousands of years of human history, it leads only to failure. Humans who are indifferent to others become isolated, and we know that we survive only when we cooperate with each other, when we take care of one another.

Hopefulness is also a unique human quality. It's our ability to visualize a better future for ourselves and our children, and to seek a happy outcome while overcoming any challenges.

Because of our ability to feel hopeful, we can say, "If John got more sleep during the day, he'd be a fine night watchman!"

And, "If I can't get these shoes from this store, I'm sure I can get them from another one."

And also, "The next time I need to write a report, I'll start earlier and avoid getting tied up in meetings."

Hopefulness allows us to say, "I have a problem today—but I can solve it tomorrow."

The opposite is despair, which says, "I have a problem today—and it cannot be solved. I'll be stuck with it forever. I have no power to change my destiny."

Which brings us back to religion and the idea of a superior or higher power. In that regard, I'm sure you have your own personal beliefs, to which you are entitled. I will only offer this: No system of belief should encourage you to be a victim or accept victimization as normal. You are a beautiful and strong human being, and you deserve a long and happy life. You are the captain of your own ship. It's your job to learn the rules of self-preservation and guide your boat along the river of life, avoiding the hazards and making good time against the current.

There's an old saying that I think applies to anyone: "God gives every bird its food, but He does not throw it into the nest." This makes me smile because it says that the world awaits you, and from its bounty you can provide for yourself and be happy—if you get out of the nest and into the world! Be trustworthy, compassionate, and hopeful. Help your neighbor, and in return you will be helped. Accept with gratitude your fair share, and leave some for the other person.

Be of good heart—and be smart!

TAKE ACTION!

- For this *Take Action!* section, I'm going to ask you to take no action—at least not now. Instead, take time to pause and reflect on your *core values*. What are they? What values of yours do you believe are non-negotiable, and why? How would you feel if you were to compromise them?

- At every step of the way, turn in the road, and door you're going to open, take a moment to ask yourself if your action will support your ethics, morals, and happiness. If you have a bad feeling, then something might be wrong. Take a moment to listen to it, figure out where it comes from, and do what you believe is right for yourself and for society. Having a clear conscience makes the rewards in life that much sweeter.

- No one expects you to have all the answers. That's just not possible! There are so many things to learn in life that you could keep yourself busy for a lifetime without ever getting bored. I wish I could cover everything in a single book, but I'm not going to try to do that—for two reasons. First, because I myself continue to learn every day; and second, because I don't want to bore you with a very long read!

- Now, I *am* going to ask you to take one more action: Ask a trusted adult for honest feedback, guidance, and sharing experiences. You can use the *5WH²* approach explained in Appendix 2 to brainstorm ideas. Once you've got that sorted, roll up your sleeves and get practical. Grab that action plan template waiting for you in Appendix 3 and start mapping out your journey to independence, self-sufficiency, and success!

Conclusion

It's Time to Hit the Road!

Thank you for reading this book!

Did you find answers to those questions you had in mind when you started? I hope so. If you're still feeling a bit stuck, it's okay.

Make an honest assessment of yourself. Take a moment to pinpoint the skills you want to develop. Again, you don't have to be good at everything, but you need to be good at *something*. It's your choice—and the options are infinite!

Meanwhile, get ready to hit the road—both literally and figuratively! If there's one thing that you and young adults your age share, it's the thrill of learning to drive and exploring the world. That's great! Because the transition to adulthood is very much like a road trip.

On a road trip, you know there will be twists, turns, bumps, and detours. When you find yourself in unfamiliar territory, you pull over to check your GPS. Eventually, you find your way.

Similarly, in the journey of adult life, you'll face ups and downs, make mistakes, and keep learning. When things become confusing and you feel a bit lost, take a break and think about what really matters to you. Check your moral compass—your *core values*—and hold on fast to them. They will be your guiding light, keeping you on the right track no matter the circumstances.

Life's paths can be unpredictable, but as an explorer, you can't just park on the side, even if it means getting a bit lost now and then. You're going to set off in search of new experiences, valuable knowledge, and a deeper understanding of the world around you.

At times, storms and rough patches might try to push you off course, but you won't abandon your ride. You'll hold on tight until things get better. Life reflects this analogy, and your values will stand as your loyal companion when life tests your courage, resilience, and determination.

So, hit the road and don't you come back no more... Unless you want to say, "Hi!"

No dream is too big. Well, hey, what's your next move?

One Last Thing...

If you believe the hard work put into this book deserves encouragement, would you mind leaving a review? Your feedback would mean the world to me as a new author and as a mom.

If you have any constructive comments, would you please share them by sending an email to ask.maya.shine@gmail.com, with "Reader Feedback" as the subject line? I'd appreciate your thoughtful insights.

If you're interested in contributing to upcoming projects about young adults, I would appreciate hearing your thoughts on topics worth considering.

Thank you for your generosity and support!

Appendix 1

Top 20 Kitchen Utensils

To cook, you need the right kitchen equipment. Of course, there are as many kitchen gadgets and tools as there are stars in the sky, but a core collection will allow you to handle essential cooking chores. Apart from the basic tableware (plates, glasses, bowls, silverware, tray, napkins), here is what you should consider on your shopping list before moving out (you can search online to see what they look like).

1. Frying pan or skillet, for making hamburgers or scrambled eggs.

2. Saucepan. This has high sides and one long handle, and usually a lid. You can fill it with water, such as for boiling your egg or cooking rice with the lid on.

3. Stock pot. This is a big saucepan, generally with two small handles, for making soups and stews.

4. Sheet pans: flat metal pans for baking cookies or heating frozen french fries in the oven.

5. Glass baking dish, for baking casseroles and enchiladas.

6. A good chef's knife. You can also buy a set. Please, watch a Youtube video to learn how to use knives. Believe me, I injured myself dozens of times before learning to chop vegetables without bleeding!

7. Measuring cup and set of spoons. You can use them for wet or dry ingredients.

8. A set of storage containers for the refrigerator and freezer.

9. Wooden mixing spoons and a ladle.

10. Spatula, for flipping pancakes and burgers.

11. Vegetable peeler.

12. Whisk, for mixing.

13. Tongs, for picking up hot items.

14. Cutting board. Make sure it's one that you can wash.

15. Colander, for draining boiled pasta and vegetables.

16. A set of nesting mixing bowls.

17. Can opener.

18. Grater, for cheese and lemon zest.

19. Blender. You might try the hand-held "stick" variety.

20. Salad spinner for drying washed lettuce or other leafy greens.

Appendix 2

Ask a Trusted Adult

*A*s you chart your roadmap to independence, seek guidance and advice from a trusted adult, whether it's your parents, guardians, or someone else who inspires you and provides you with a sense of security. Remember, they've walked the same path so make the most of their wisdom.

In Chapter 1, "Know Yourself," we discussed the importance of the 5WH² method in the introspection process. Now, let's apply this invaluable toolkit more expansively. Here are some questions you can ask a trusted adult to brainstorm ideas on the skills you need to develop:

1. What do you think I'm strong at?

    This question can help you identify your strengths and talents, which can be the foundation for your future endeavors (review Chapter 1).

2. What skill do you think I should improve or learn?

    Ask about skills that might be valuable in adulthood. Then delve deeper by asking:

    - Why should I learn it?
    - How did you manage to learn it?

- How do you think I should learn it?
- Can you help me?
- Where did you learn it?
- When did you learn it?

These follow-up questions not only provide guidance, but also actionable steps you can include in your action plan (refer to the template in Appendix 3).

3. When you were my age and wanted to strike out on your own, what challenges did you face, and how did you manage to overcome them?

    Learning from someone else's experiences can be incredibly valuable. Then ask:

4. What would you have done differently and why?

    This question allows you to learn from others' mistakes, the lessons they've learned, and the pitfalls you should avoid. I believe there's nothing more enriching than experience sharing. It also allows you to take shortcuts, and who doesn't like a good shortcut?

    More specifically, you can ask the following questions:

5. How much money should I aim to save before moving out on my own or pursuing higher education?

6. How much should I budget for living expenses, including rent, utilities, groceries, and transportation, when I start living on my own?

7. What are some common financial mistakes young adults make, and how can I avoid them?

8. Who can provide guidance on building a strong credit history, and how can I responsibly manage credit?

9. Where can I find reliable sources of financial education and advice for young adults, and what might the associated costs be?

10. When it comes to career decisions, what challenges did you face at my age, and how did you overcome them?

11. What investments, such as education or training, did you need to make to get your job, and how much did they cost?

12. What would you have done differently in terms of financial planning and career choices, and why?

By using the *5WH²* approach, you'll establish a structured method for gathering advice and insights from trusted adults. Integrating the "*How much*" aspect into these questions will provide you with practical information for budgeting and financial planning, which are essential for a successful transition into self-sufficient adulthood.

Appendix 3

Action Plan Template

Once you have identified the skills you want to develop or strengthen, in Appendix 2, take a moment to determine which ones can help you reach your goals, making your dreams a reality. Then, create your action plan.

Reflect on Your Action Plan

Personally, as I get ready to step into the unknown, I embrace the power of preparation, using the 5WH^2 method. This not only ensures a comprehensive approach to gathering information, but also gives me the ability to see the big picture, organize my thoughts, foresee challenges, and figure out the necessary actions. The more I prepare, the more confident I feel. Even if there's still a little bit of stress, that's okay because it's not holding me back; on the contrary, it pushes me forward. This positive stress keeps me sharp, alert, and fully engaged in the exciting journey ahead.

This section presents introspective questions for you to think about your action plan. I hope this moment of reflection will help you find your path.

1. What: Identify Goals	2. Why: Establish Purpose
• What do you want to accomplish? • What are your goals for preparing to move out on your own? • What specific life skills do you need to develop to achieve your goals?	• Why do you want to accomplish these goals? • Why do you want to move out on your own? • Why is it important for you to learn these skills?
3. How: Take Action Steps and Budget	**4.a Who: Identify Support**
• How will you go about learning each skill? • How will you research opportunities and resources?	• Who can provide guidance and support in acquiring these skills? • Who are the trusted adults or mentors you can turn to for advice?
	4.b What: Identify Resources
	• What resources do you need to learn these skills?
5. Where: Locate Resources and Support	**6. How Much: Budget and Plan Finances**
• Where can you find the resources and support you need to learn these skills?	• How much money do you need to learn these skills? • How much can you allocate for skill development?

7. When: Set Timelines	8. Monitor and Evaluate
• When do you want to achieve each skill or milestone? • When do you plan to move out on your own?	• Regularly track your progress achieving each milestone. • Evaluate your budget and financial plan periodically to ensure you're on track.
9. Adjust and Revise	**10. Seek Guidance and Feedback**
• Be flexible and make adjustments to your plan if needed.	• Continue to consult with trusted adults or mentors for guidance, feedback and assistance in facing challenges.
11. Celebrate Milestones	**12. Review and Reflect**
• Acknowledge your achievements along the way to stay motivated. Celebrate each success! You deserve to be happy!	• Reflect on your progress and experiences regularly to enhance your learning. • Embrace life's challenges and experiences as valuable opportunities for personal growth and learning.

Monitor Your Progress

If you like planning and being well-organized, consider using the table in this section to track your progress toward your goals. Fictional examples are included; you can use a tool as basic as Excel or as advanced as project management software.

It's worth noting that action plans are widely used in the workplace, and the more you get used to planning your tasks, the more efficient you'll become at optimizing your time and resources, whether in your professional or personal life. Besides, being well-organized saves you time, and time is money!

Columns Description:

- **Life Skill to Learn:** List the specific life skills you want to learn or strengthen.
- **Desired Outcome:** Identify the goal you want to achieve through learning a skill.
- **Actions:** Break down your goal into smaller and manageable tasks.
- **Required Resources:** Identify the resources, materials, courses, mentors, or support you need and where to find these.
- **Budget:** Determine the cost of the resources you need.
- **Start:** Note the date when you begin working on each skill.
- **End:** Set a target date for when you plan to complete each action.
- **Status:** Note whether a particular action has been completed, is in progress, is pending, or if there are any issues or obstacles associated with it.
- **Challenges:** Note any difficulties, obstacles, or challenges faced. Talk to trusted adults for guidance on how to overcome them. If necessary, adjust your action plan.
- **Celebrate Success:** It may seem ordinary, but you should never underestimate your accomplishments, no matter how small they may be. Celebrate your success each time you accomplish a milestone (action). It can be as simple as treating yourself to a tasty snack or congratulating yourself while looking in the mirror. Not that expensive, but so fulfilling!
- **Lessons learned:** Note what you've learned from your experiences and prepare to become a *trusted adult* for someone else!

My Success Story

Life Skill 1 (What): Financial Literacy

Desired Outcome (Why): To develop a strong understanding of personal finance and make informed financial decisions

Actions (How)	Resources (What)	Resources (Who)	Resources (Where)	Budget (How much)	Start (When)	End (When)	Status	Challenges	Celebrate Success	Lessons Learned
Meet with a Financial Advisor	-	Financial Advisor	Local Bank Branch	Free	[Date]	[Date]	Done	Finding time	Have a nice dinner	Financial planning is essential
Open a Savings Account	-	Financial Advisor	Local Bank Branch	Free	[Date]	[Date]	On Hold	Meeting minimum balance		
Consult with an Accountant	-	Accountant	Local Clinic	$50	[Date]	[Date]	Done	Navigating tax laws	Watch favorite movie	Importance of professional advice
Create a Monthly Budget Spreadsheet	Excel	Me	At home	Free	[Date]	[Date]	Done	Tracking expenses	Meal with friends	Importance of managing expenses for financial control

My Success Story

Life Skill 2 (What): Cooking
Desired Outcome (Why): To eat healthy food and save more money each month

Actions (How)	Resources (What)	Resources (Who)	Resources (Where)	Budget (How much)	Start (When)	End (When)	Status	Challenges	Celebrate Success	Lessons Learned
Read cookbooks & Explore the Mediterranean diet	Cookbooks	-	Library, Online	Free	[Date]	[Date]	Done	Finding time	Buy a personal recipe journal	Plus Value of self-discipline and self-study
Attend cooking workshops	Workshops	-	Community Center	$200	[Date]	[Date]	Done	Chopping veggies safely	Host a potluck gathering	Benefits of cooking
Seek mentorship from an experienced cook	-	Anna	Community Center	Free	[Date]	[Date]	In progress	None	Prepare a special dinner	Benefits of mentorship

My Success Story

Life Skill 3 (What): Improve my ability to memorize my lessons using the SQ3R method
Desired Outcome (Why): To enhance my learning experience and retention of study material, to graduate

Actions (How)	Resources (What)	Resources (Who)	Resources (Where)	Budget (How much)	Start (When)	End (When)	Status	Challenges	Celebrate Success	Lessons Learned
Survey: Prior to in-depth study, quickly skim the lesson material to get an overview.	Pen paper timer	Self-study	Quiet study place	Free	[Date]	[Date]	In progress	Staying focused	Home-made memory-boosting smoothie	Importance of active engagement in the learning process
Question: Formulate questions about the content to focus on key points.	Pen paper timer	Self-study	Quiet study place	Free	[Date]	[Date]	In progress	Formulating effective questions for each lesson	Meditation & relaxation break	Importance of setting study goals & questions
Read: Read the material carefully while actively reciting key points out loud.	Pen paper timer	Self-study	Quiet study place	Free	[Date]	[Date]	Not Started		Walk or exercise session	
Recite: Summarize and explain the material in my own words.	Pen paper timer	Self-study	Quiet study place	Free	[Date]	[Date]	Not Started		Mindfulness exercise	
Review: Regularly review the material to reinforce my memory.	Pen paper timer	Self-study	Quiet study place	Free	[Date]	[Date]	Not Started		Favorite artistic activity	

Endnotes

1   SWNS Staff, "81% of Recent College Grads Wish They Were Taught More Life Skills Before Graduation," *SWNS Digital*, October 4, 2021, https://swns digital.com/us/2021/07/eighty-one-percent-of-recent-college-graduates-wish-they-were-taught-more-life-skills-before-graduating/

2   Dana Wilkie, "Employer's Say Students Aren't Learning Soft Skills in College," *SHRM*, October 21, 2019, https://www.shrm.org/resourcesandtools/hr-topics/employee-relations/pages/employers-say-students-arent-learning-soft-skills-in-college.aspx

3   Tom Huddleston Jr., "What Microsoft Billionaire Bill Gates Was Doing at 20 Years Old," CNBC: Make It, March 29, 2018, https://www.cnbc.com/2018/

03/29/what-microsoft-billionaire-bill-gates-was-doing-at-20-years-old.html

4   StrategyPunk Staff, "5W1H Method: Unlocking the Secrets of Effective Problem Solving," *StrategyPunk*, March 23, 2023, https://www.strategypunk.com/5w1h-method-unlocking-the-secrets-of-effective-problem-solving/

5   Dr. Carol S. Dweck, *Mindset: The New Psychology of Success* (New York: Random House, 2007)

6   4BC Radio Brisbane Interview with Dr. Norman Doidge, *Sonic Learning*, February 7, 2012, https://soniclearning.com.au/dr-norman-doidge-interviewed-on-4bc-radio-brisbane/

7   Courtney E. Ackerman, M.A., "What is Neuroplasticity? A Psychologist Explains," Positive Psychology, July 25, 2018, https://positivepsychology.com/neuroplasticity/#:~:text=The%20term%20%E2%80%9Cneuroplasticity%E2%80%9D%20was%20first,widely%20used%20until%20the%201960s

8   4BC Radio Brisbane Interview with Dr. Norman Doidge, Sonic Learning, February 7, 2012, https://soniclearning.com.au/dr-norman-doidge-interviewed-on-4bc-radio-brisbane/

9   Norman Doidge, M.D., *The Brain that Changes Itself: Stories of Personal Triumph from the Frontiers of Brain Science* (New York: Penguin, 2007)

10 Tim Adams, "Norman Doidge: the Man Teaching Us to Change Our Minds," The Guardian, February 8, 2015, https://www.theguardian.com/science/2015/feb/08/norman-doidge-brain-healing-neuroplasticity-interview

11 Tom Williams for Utah Public Radio, "The Brain that Changes Itself," *UPR: Morning Edition*, March 16, 2015, https://www.upr.org/programs/2015-03-16/the-brain-that-changes-itself-on-mondays-access-utah

12 Suzana Herculano-Houzel, "The Human Brain in Numbers: A Linearly Scaled-up Primate Brain." *Frontiers in Human Neuroscience*, November 9, 2009, https://www.ncbi.nlm.nih.gov/pmc/articles/PMC2776484/ doi: 10.33.89/neuro.09.031.2009

13 Maggie Masetti, "How Many Stars in the Milky Way?," National Aeronautics and Space Administration, *NASA: Blueshift*, July 22, 2015, https://asd.gsfc.nasa.gov/blueshift/index.php/2015/07/22/how-many-stars-in-the-milky-way/

14 Tim Adams, "Norman Doidge: the Man Teaching Us to Change Our Minds," The Guardian, February 8, 2015, https://www.theguardian.com/science/2015/feb/08/norman-doidge-brain-healing-neuroplasticity-interview

15 Guy Raz with Suzana Herculano-Houzel, "What Makes the Human Brain

Endnotes

Unique?" *NPR: TED Radio Hour*, February 20, 2015, https://www.npr.org/
transcripts/384949670#:~:text=HERCULANO%2DHOUZEL%3A%20
We%20found%20an,are%20an%20entire%20baboon%20brain

16 V.J. Felitti et. al., "Relationship of Childhood Abuse and Household Dysfunc-
tion to Many of the Leading Causes of Death in Adults. The Adverse Childhood Experiences (ACE) Study. *American Journal of Preventive Medicine*. 1998
May;14(4):245-58. doi: 10.1016/s0749-3797(98)00017-8. PMID: 9635069,
https://pubmed.ncbi.nlm.nih.gov/9635069/

17 If you have been affected by ACE and want to learn more about the compel-
ling advances in this field, Bessel van der Kolk's *New York Times'* best-selling,
The Body Keeps the Score provides a highly accessible introduction. Bessel van
der Kolk, M.D., *The Body Keeps the Score: Brain, Mind, and Body, in the Heal-
ing of Trauma*, (New York: Penguin Books, 2015)

18 Laura Starecheski, "Take the ACE Quiz And Learn What It Does–And
Doesn't Mean," *NPR*, March 2, 2015, https://www.npr.org/sections/health-
shots/2015/03/02/387007941/take-the-ace-quiz-and-learn-what-it-does-and-
doesnt-mean

19 Reuters Staff, "More Than Half the World Will be Obese by 2035, Report
Predicts," CNN, March 3, 2023, https://www.cnn.com/2023/03/03/world/
world-obesity-2023-wellness-intl-scli/index.html#:~:text=The%20World%20
Obesity%20Federation's%202023,income%20countries%2C%20the%20
report%20found

20 Aakash K. Patel, Vamsi Reddy, Karlie R. Shumway, John F. Arujo, "Physiology,
Sleep Stages," *StatPearls*, September 7, 2022, https://www.ncbi.nlm.nih.gov/
books/NBK526132/#:~:text=Sleep%20occurs%20in%20five%20stages,stage
%20a%20progressively%20deeper%20sleep

21 Whitney Sleep Center Staff, "5 Stages of Sleep," *Whitney Sleep Center*, April 27,
2021, https://whitneysleepcenter.com/blog/5-stages-of-sleep/#:~:text=Stage%
202%3A%20Non%2DREM%20Sleep,and%20unaware%20of%20your%20
surroundings

22 Eric Suni and Abnihav Singh, M.D., "Stages of Sleep: What Happens in a
Sleep Cycle," *Sleep Foundation*, November 3, 2023, https://www.sleepfoundation
.org/stages-of-sleep

23 National Heart, Lung, and Blood Initiative, "Sleep Phases and Stages," How
Sleep Works, March 24, 2022, https://www.nhlbi.nih.gov/health/sleep/stages-
of-sleep#:~:text=The%20cycle%20starts%20over%20every,classify%20sleep
%20phases%20and%20stages

24   Danice K. Eaton, Ph.D., et. al. "Prevalence of Insufficient, Borderline, and Optimal Hours of Sleep Among High School Students–United States, 2007," *Journal of Adolescent Health*, 46, no. 4 (April 2010): 399-401, https://www.jahonline.org/article/S1054-139X%2809%2900600-4/fulltext

25   Division of Population Health, National Center for Chronic Disease Prevention and Health Promotion, "Sleep in Middle and High School," *CDC*, September 10, 2020.

26   Ruthann Richter, "Among Teens, Sleep Deprivation an Epidemic," *Stanford Medicine: News Center*, October 8, 2015, https://med.stanford.edu/news/all-news/2015/10/among-teens-sleep-deprivation-an-epidemic.html

27   Juliann Garey, "Teens and Sleep: The Cost of Sleep Deprivation," *Child Mind Institute*, October 30, 2023, https://childmind.org/article/happens-teenagers-dont-get-enough-sleep/

28   Newport Academy Staff, "Sleep Deprivation in Teens," *Newport Academy: Well-being*, January 7, 2022, https://www.newportacademy.com/resources/well-being/sleep-deprived-teens/

29   Ruthmann Richter, "Among Teens, Sleep Deprivation an Epidemic," *Stanford Medicine News Center*, October 8, 2023, https://med.stanford.edu/news/all-news/2015/10/among-teens-sleep-deprivation-an-epidemic.html

30   Cleveland Clinic Staff, "Why You Should Ditch Your Phone Before Bed," *Cleveland Clinic: Health Essentials*, May 20, 2022, https://health.clevelandclinic.org/put-the-phone-away-3-reasons-why-looking-at-it-before-bed-is-a-bad-habit/

31   Christopher Drake, et al., "Caffeine Effects on Sleep Taken 0, 3, or 6 Hours Before Going to Bed," *Journal of Clinical Sleep Medicine*, November, 2013, https://www.ncbi.nlm.nih.gov/pmc/articles/PMC3805807/ doi: 10.5664/jcsm.3170

32   Mayo Clinic Staff, "Caffeine: How Much is Too Much?" *Mayo Clinic: Healthy Lifestyle*, March 19, 2022, https://www.mayoclinic.org/healthy-lifestyle/nutrition-and-healthy-eating/in-depth/caffeine/art-20045678

33   Deirdre Conroy, M.D., "When to Stop Drinking Alcohol, Water, or Caffeine Before Bed for Better Sleep," *Michigan Medicine*, University of Michigan, December 16, 2020, https://medicine.umich.edu/dept/psychiatry/news/archive/202012/when-stop-drinking-alcohol-water-or-caffeine-bed-better-sleep#:~:text=%22But%20in%20general%2C%20our%20guideline,should%20eliminate%20all%20caffeinated%20products.%22&text=alcohol%20before%20bed-,Dr

34   U.S. Bureau of Labor Statistics, "Earnings and Unemployment Rates by Edu-

cational Attainment, 2022," *USBLS*, September 6, 2023, https://www.bls.gov/emp/chart-unemployment-earnings-education.htm

35 Steve Gorman, "Billionaire Branson Soars to Space Aboard Virgin Galactic Flight," *Reuters*, July 12, 2021, https://www.reuters.com/lifestyle/science/virgin-galactics-branson-ready-space-launch-aboard-rocket-plane-2021-07-11/

36 Sky News Staff, "Virgin Galactic's First Commercial Space Flight Launches–What Happens On Board and How Much Are Tickets?," *Sky News*, June 29, 2023, https://news.sky.com/story/virgin-galactics-first-commercial-space-flight-is-set-to-take-off-what-will-happen-on-board-and-how-much-are-tickets-12911100

37 Selena Hill, "Born Into Slavery, This Centenarian Learned to Read at 116, Becoming the Nation's Oldest Student," *Black Enterprise*, January 3, 2020, https://www.blackenterprise.com/meet-former-slave-learned-to-read-116-mary-walker/

38 IMSE Journal Staff, "12 Famous People Who Struggled with Dyslexia Before Changing the World," *IMSE Journal*, November 21, 2017, https://journal.imse.com/12-famous-people-who-struggled-with-dyslexia-before-changing-the-world/

39 Francis P. Robinson, *Effective Study*, (New York: Harper & Brothers, 1946)

40 Ali Montag, "Jay Leno Learned this Life Lesson from a Pair of Mystery Underwear he Found Working at McDonald's," *CNBC: Make It*, May 7, 2018, https://www.cnbc.com/2018/05/07/what-working-at-mcdonalds-taught-jay-leno-about-success.html

41 Rachel Sugar, "From Selling Bras to Taming Lions, Here are the Summer Jobs 19 Super Successful People Had Before They Were Famous," *Insider*, July 3, 2015, https://www.businessinsider.com/super-successful-peoples-summer-jobs-2015-7#news-anchor-anderson-cooper-interned-at-the-cia-11111116

42 Robert D. Austin and Gary P.Pisano, "Neurodiversity as a Competitive Advantage," *Harvard Business Review*, May-June 2017, https://hbr.org/2017/05/neurodiversity-as-a-competitive-advantage

43 Tom Huddleston Jr., "Founder of 1-800-GOT-JUNK? Dropped out of College to Haul Junk–Now, He's Eyeing a Billion-Dollar Business," *CNBC: Make It*, August 1, 2020, https://www.cnbc.com/2020/08/01/how-the-1-800-got-junk-founder-became-a-multimillionaire.html#:~:text=billion%2Ddollar%20business-,Founder%20of%201%2D800%2DGOT%2DJUNK%3F,eyeing%

20a%20billion%2Ddollar%20business&text=Tom%20Huddleston%20Jr.&
text=Inspiration%20can%20strike%20at%20any%20moment

44 Madeline Berg, "Dolly Parton's Net Worth Revealed: The Staggering Success of
America's Country Music Queen," *Forbes* August 5, 2021,https://www.forbes.
com/sites/maddieberg/2021/08/05/dolly-partons-net-worth-revealed-the-
staggering-success-of-americas-country-music-queen/?sh=36873dde6a28

45 Olivia Perkins, *IRS Audits Low-Income Taxpayers More Often than Wealthier Peers,
Study Finds," Signal Cleveland,* March 10, 2023, https://signalcleveland.org/irs-
audits-low-income-taxpayers-more-often-than-wealthier-peers-study-finds/

46 Melania Hanson, "Average Student Loan Debt," Educational Data Initiative,
May 22, 2023, https://educationdata.org/average-student-loan-debt

47 Federal Trade Commission, "Get a Vehicle's History," Used Cars, November 5,
2018, https://consumer.ftc.gov/features/used-cars#:~:text=Breadcrumb&text=
If%20you're%20buying%20a,ever%20was%20declared%20as%20salvage

48 Venkatesh Elango, "Who Owns a Car in New York?," *GitHub Inc.,* June 20,
2021, https://wellango.github.io/posts/2021/06/who-owns-cars-in-nyc/

49 Nathan Paulus, "Car Ownership in the US," *MoneyGeek,* March 16, 2023,
https://www.moneygeek.com/insurance/auto/car-ownership-statistics/#:~:text=
Show%20more-,Vehicle%20Ownership%20By%20City,of%201.63%20cars%
20per%20household

50 University of Philadelphia School of Engineering, Philadelphia, PA, "Vehicle
Stopping Distance and Time," National Association of City Transportation
Officials, September 17, 2013, https://nacto.org/docs/usdg/vehicle_stopping_
distance_and_time_upenn.pdf

51 The Zebra Staff, "Drowsy Driving Statistics," *The Zebra,* January 31, 2023,
https://www.thezebra.com/resources/research/drowsy-driving-statistics/

52 DriversEd Staff, "What is a Tire Blow Out, and How Do I Handle One?"
DriversEd, March 31, 2022, https://driversed.com/trending/what-tire-blow-
out-and-how-do-i-handle-one#:~:text=A%20tire%20blowout%20occurs%20
when,tire%20pressure%20being%20too%20low

53 NHTSA, "Passenger Vehicle Occupant Fatalities by Day and Night–A Contrast," May, 2007, chrome-extension://efaidnbmnnnibpcajpcglclefindmkaj/
https://crashstats.nhtsa.dot.gov/Api/Public/ViewPublication/810637

54 Adiel Kaplan, Jean Lee, Joe Enoch, Vicky Nguyen, "Blinded by the Light: Cars
in the U.S. Still Lack Glare-Reducing Headlights, May 11, 2023, https://www.
nbcnews.com/news/us-news/blinded-light-american-headlight-safety-lags-

years-countries-rcna82666

55 Jiffy Lube Staff, "High Beam vs. Low Beam," *Car Lights and Glass*, https://www.jiffylube.com/resource-center/high-beam-vs-low-beam

56 Taylor Auto Glass Staff, "High Beam Safety Tips," *Driving Tips: Vehicle Safety*, June 22, 2018, https://taylorautoglass.com/high-beam-safety-tips/#:~:text=Instead%2C%20try%20to%20look%20at,other%20driver%20isn't%20safe!

57 National Safety Council Staff, "The Most Dangerous Time to Drive, *NSC: Road Safety*, 2023, https://www.nsc.org/road/safety-topics/driving-at-night

58 International Science Council, "Cycling Towards Sustainable Development," March 6, 2023, *ISC Online*, https://council.science/current/blog/cycling-towards-sustainable-development/

59 United Nations, "General Assembly Unanimously Adopts Texts on Combating Islamophobia, Protecting Rangelands, Tackling Difficulties for Widows, Bicycles as Public Transportation," *UN: Meetings Coverage and Press Releases*, General Assembly Seventy-sixth Session, March 12, 2022, https://press.un.org/en/2022/ga12408.doc.htm

60 Khristopher J. Brooks, "Here's the Age When Most Americans Buy Their First Home," *CBS News*, November 4, 2022, https://www.cbsnews.com/news/first-time-homebuyer-age-realtor-data/

61 *Justin Pritchard, "Where Do You Park Your Car Keys? Preventing Relay Attacks," Driver, November 5, 2021*

62 Nils-Gerrit Wunsch, "Cooking Practices of Millennials and Generation Z in the U.S. and Canada in 2022," *Statista*, April 2022, https://www.statista.com/statistics/1309600/north-america-young-adults-cooking-practices/

63 Unazia Faizan & Audra S. Rouster, "Nutrition and Hydration Requirements in Children and Adults," Treasure Island, FL: *StatPearls* Publishing, January 2023, https://www.ncbi.nlm.nih.gov/books/NBK562207/

64 Study by Kelton for the American Gastroentological Association, "New Study Finds Forty Percent of Americans' Daily Lives are Disrupted by Digestive Troubles," *AGA*, September 14, 2022, https://gastro.org/press-releases/new-survey-finds-forty-percent-of-americans-daily-lives-are-disrupted-by-digestive-troubles/

65 *Drew Desilver, "What Data Says About Food Stamps in the U.S.," Pew Research Center, July 19, 2023, https://www.pewresearch.org/short-reads/2023/07/19/what-the-data-says-about-food-stamps-in-the-u-s/*

66 *National Council on Aging, "Where Can I Use SNAP Benefits?" NCO Online,* November 5, 2021, https://www.ncoa.org/article/where-can-i-use-snap-benefits

67 Alisha Coleman-Jensen and Matthew P. Rabbit, "Food Pantry Use Increased in 2020 for Most Types of U.S. Households," U.S. Department of Agriculture: *Amber Waves*, November 8, 2021, https://www.ers.usda.gov/amber-waves/2021/november/food-pantry-use-increased-in-2020-for-most-types-of-u-s-households/

68 Bédard, Alexandra et al. "Can eating pleasure be a lever for healthy eating? A systematic scoping review of eating pleasure and its links with dietary behaviors and health." PloS one vol. 15,12 e0244292. 21 Dec. 2020, doi:10.1371/journal.pone.0244292

69 Ancel Benjamin Keys, *How to Eat Well and Stay Well the Mediterranean Way* (New York: Doubleday, 1975)

70 Mayo Clinic Staff, "Mediterranean Diet for Heart Health," Mayo Clinic Online: Healthy Lifestyle, https://www.mayoclinic.org/healthy-lifestyle/nutrition-and-healthy-eating/in-depth/mediterranean-diet/art-20047801#:~:text=Today%2C%20the%20Mediterranean%20diet%20is,as%20a%20healthy%2Deating%20pattern

71 Chelsea van Bloom and Maria McGinnis, "What's the Best Refrigerator Temperature?" U.S. & World Report News, August 21, 2023, https://www.usnews.com/360-reviews/home-goods/refrigerators/best-temperature#:~:text=What%20Is%20the%20Best%20Temperature%20for%20My%20Refrigerator%3F&text=The%20ideal%20refrigerator%20temperature%20is,coli

72 Renee Onque,, "2023's 'Dirty Dozen': the 12 Fruits and Vegetables with the Most Pesticides—and Four Tips for Enjoying them Safely," CNBC: Make It, March 29, 2023, https://www.cnbc.com/2023/03/29/dirty-dozen-2023-12-fruits-and-vegetables-with-the-most-pesticides.html

73 CDC, "Fruit and Vegetable Safety," *CDC Online: Foods That Can Cause Food Poisoning*, https://www.cdc.gov/foodsafety/communication/steps-healthy-fruits-veggies.html

74 Arm & Hammer, "Get Cleaner Fruits and Vegetables with Baking Soda," Arm & Hammer Online, https://www.armandhammer.com/articles/how-to-clean-fruits-and-vegetables#:~:text=For%20a%20mixing%20bowl%2C%20add,for%2012%20to%2015%20minutes

75 FDA, "Outbreak Examination of E. Coli: Romaine from Salinas, California (November 2019), FDA Online Investigation Report, May 21, 2020, https://www.fda.gov/food/outbreaks-foodborne-illness/outbreak-investigation-e-coli-romaine-salinas-california-november-2019#:~:text=May%2021%2C%202020,during%20the%20Fall%20of%202019

76 Feeding America, "Food Waste and Food Rescue," Feeding America Online, https://www.feedingamerica.org/our-work/reduce-food-waste#:~:text=Shockingly%2C%20nearly%2040%25%20of%20all,billion%20pounds%20of%20food%20waste

77 Move for Hunger, "What is Hunger?," *Move for Hunger Online,* 2023, https://moveforhunger.org/hunger-facts?gclid=Cj0KCQiAjMKqBhCgARIsAPDgWlwKdF1NDkDDj15M31rYPiu6W2EDVWLCVGgzmKaYr6R5_-TlMdTPICAaAizwEALw_wcB

78 Katherine Zeratsky, R.D., L.D., "Nutrition and Healthy Eating," Mayo Clinic: *Healthy Eating,* October 4, 2022, https://www.mayoclinic.org/healthy-lifestyle/nutrition-and-healthy-eating/expert-answers/food-safety/faq-20058500

79 United States Department of Agriculture, "Leftovers and Food Safety," USDA Online: Food Safety and Inspection Service, https://www.fsis.usda.gov/food-safety/safe-food-handling-and-preparation/food-safety-basics/leftovers-and-food-safety#:~:text=When%20thawing%20leftovers%20in%20a,it%20to%20this%20safe%20temperature

80 T.K. Logan and Robert Walker, "The Gender Safety Gap: Examining the Impact of Victimization History, Perceived Risk, and Personal Control," Sage Journals, Vol. 36, Issue 1-2, September 4, 2017, https://journals.sagepub.com/doi/full/10.1177/0886260517729405

81 M E Lewyn, "Men, Women, and Crime," San Diego Justice Journal, Vol. 1, Issue 1, (Winter 1993), pp. 57-64, https://www.ojp.gov/ncjrs/virtual-library/abstracts/men-women-and-crime

82 United Nations Office on Drugs and Crime, "Global Study on Homicide: Gender-related Killing of Women and Girls, Vienna: UNDOC Research, 2018, https://www.unodc.org/documents/data-and-analysis/GSH2018/GSH18_Gender-related_killing_of_women_and_girls.pdf

83 KMD Law, "Why Sexual Abuse Survivors are Afraid to Speak Up," Rape, Abuse & Incest National Network, July 7, 2021, https://www.kmdlaw.com/blog/2021/july/why-sexual-assault-survivors-are-afraid-to-speak/

84 Care Net Staff, "Date Rape Facts You Need to Know," Care Net Online: Pregnancy Centers of Albequerque, December 15, 2021, https://carenetabq.com/date-rape-facts-you-need-to-know/#:~:text=Date%20rape%20affects%2035%20percent,you%20know%20%E2%80%93%20is%20never%20OK

85 Jack M. Germain, "Young Adults, Seniors Over 75 Most Susceptible to Cyber Fraud," TechNewsWorld, March 18, 2021, https://www.technewsworld.com/

story/young-adults-seniors-over-75-most-susceptible-to-cyber-fraud-report-87059.html

86 Kspersky Staff, "What is WannaCry Ransomeware?" Kapersky Online, 2023, https://www.kaspersky.com/resource-center/threats/ransomware-wannacry

87 William L. Hosch, "Zombie Computer," Britannica Online: History & Society, August 29, 2023, https://www.britannica.com/technology/zombie-computer

88 Malwarebytes Staff, "All About Spyware," Malwarebytes, https://www.malware-bytes.com/spyware

89 Safety Detective Staff, "7 Best Spyware Protection Software in 2023," Safety Detective Online, November 10, 2023, https://www.safetydetective.com/recommended2/best-spyware-protection-2/?cq_src=google_ads&cq_cmp=2061 3825965&cq_term=spyware+protection+software&cq_plac=&cq_net=g&cq_plt=gp&gclid=CjwKCAiAxreqBhAxEiwAfGfndHpxvDcYE3gfX-iXe8LcUa7LsK bRDNjbE2T9258YZulWrieV1RUElBoCmVgQAvD_BwE

90 Javelin Strategy & Research, "Identity Fraud Losses Totalled $43 Billion in 2022, Affecting 40 Million U.S. Adults," *Javelin*, March 28, 2023, https://javelinstrategy.com/press-release/identity-fraud-losses-totaled-43-billion-2022-affecting-40-million-us-adults

91 Noah Rosenberg, "28 Indicted in Theft of Steakhouse Patrons' Credit Card Data," *The New York Times*, November 18, 2011, https://www.nytimes.com/2011/11/19/nyregion/28-indicted-in-theft-of-credit-card-data-at-steakhouses.html

92 FBI: Press Office, "Internet Crime Complaint Center Releases 2022 Statistics," FBI Online, March 22, 2023, https://www.fbi.gov/contact-us/field-offices/springfield/news/internet-crime-complaint-center-releases-2022-statistics#:~:text=Phishing%20schemes%20were%20the%20number,citizens%20aged%2060%20and%20older

93 Emery Winter, "Yes, Scammers Call People and Ask 'Can You Hear Me?'" Verify, September 8, 2023, https://www.verifythis.com/article/news/verify/scams-verify/can-you-hear-me-say-yes-robocall-phone-call-spam-scam/536-8f73483d-165a-4c51-88d1-7581c6a043c6

94 Office of the Minnesota Attorney General Keith Ellison, "'Can You Hear Me?' Scam Calls," https://www.ag.state.mn.us/consumer/Publications/CanYouHearMe.asp